The Giant Book of Weird Facts

By
Jake Jacobs

Kindle Edition

* * * * *

Published by Jake Jacobs at Amazon Kindle

The Giant Book of Weird Facts
Copyright© 2018 by Jake Jacobs

1.

Gorillas compose songs that they hum or sing during mealtimes, according to a study of wild western lowland gorillas in the Republic of the Congo.

Reference: (https://www.newscientist.com/article/2078781-wild-gorillas-compose-happy-songs-that-they-hum-during-meals/)

2.

The Law of Urination states that all mammals, regardless of size, take the same time to urinate, which is about 20 seconds.

Reference: (http://voices.nationalgeographic.com/2013/10/23/new-law-of-urination-mammals-take-21-seconds-to-pee/)

3.

North Korea lost 50 submarines and then found them.

Reference: (https://news.vice.com/article/north-koreas-50-missing-submarines-have-apparently-reappeared-following-truce)

4.

AIDS was originally called GRID, which stood for the Gay Related Immune Deficiency.

Reference: (http://www.nytimes.com/1982/05/11/science/new-homosexual-disorder-worries-health-officials.html?pagewanted)

5.

San Diego's, La Jolla seaside cliffs, are eroding at a record pace while the coastal multi-million dollar homes are unable to receive home owners insurance and face city fines of $500,000 when they inevitably collapse into the Pacific Ocean.

Reference: (http://www.sandiego.gov/development-services/pdf/hearingofficer/reports/2015/HO-15-015.pdf)

6.

Author Janet Frame, after being diagnosed with schizophrenia, had scheduled a lobotomy. Days before the procedure, she won a national literary prize. The procedure was cancelled.

Reference: (http://www.nytimes.com/2004/01/30/books/janet-frame-79-writer-who-explored-madness.html?_r=0)

7.

In 1938, 18-year-old Korean Yang Kyoungjong was conscripted by Japan to fight against the USSR. In 1939, he was captured by the Soviets and sent to fight against the Germans. He was then captured by the Nazis and sent to fight on D-Day only to be captured by the Americans.

Reference: (https://en.wikipedia.org/wiki/Yang_Kyoungjong)

8.

Greenland's economy relies almost entirely on the fishing industry and Danish Government support.

Reference:
(http://www.economywatch.com/world_economy/greenland/)

9.

There's an analog to the laser that emits sound. It's called the Saser, and it's been around for less than a decade.

Reference:(https://en.wikipedia.org/wiki/Sound_amplification_by_stimulated_emission_of_radiation)

10.

The U.S. has had a Native American vice president.

Reference: (https://en.wikipedia.org/wiki/Charles_Curtis)

11.

When George R.R. Martin was young, he wrote stories about a mythical kingdom populated by his pet turtles. The turtles died frequently in their toy castle, so he finally decided they were killing each other off in "sinister plots".

Reference:
(https://en.wikipedia.org/wiki/George_R._R._Martin#Biography)

12.

Princeton was the last Ivy League college to admit a black student in 1947. That was 90 years after Yale admitted its first black student in 1857.

Reference: (https://www.jbhe.com/chronology/)

13.

"Roko's Basilisk" is a hypothetical, all-powerful artificial intelligence from the future which may retroactively punish those who had not helped to bring about its existence and that by simply knowing about the Basilisk opens you up to punishment.

Reference: (http://rationalwiki.org/wiki/Roko's_basilisk)

14.

John F. Kennedy won the United States Presidency by only a 0.17% margin.

Reference:
(https://en.wikipedia.org/wiki/United_States_presidential_election,_1960)

15.

Hitler was a vegetarian and when he was at social events, he would share graphic accounts of the slaughter of animals in an effort to make his dinner guests shun meat.

Reference: (https://en.wikipedia.org/wiki/Adolf_Hitler#Health)

16.

As Romance and Germanic languages are related, the Romance p- and c- often corresponds to the Germanic f- and h- respectively.

Reference: (https://en.wikipedia.org/wiki/Indo-European_languages#Sound_changes/)

17.

Bruce Springsteen never had a number 1 single on the Billboard Top 100.

Reference: (http://www.clashmusic.com/feature/10-things-you-never-knew-about-bruce-springsteen)

18.

Giraffes can last longer without drinking water than camels.

Reference: (http://www.oliversozone.com/blog/which-animals-can-last-the-longest-without-water/)

19.

The deadliest air-raid in history occurred on March 9th, 1945. 330 American B-29 Super-fortresses dropped incendiary bombs on Tokyo, touching off a firestorm that killed over 100,000 people. The raid burned a quarter of the city to the ground and left over a million people homeless.

Reference:
(https://en.wikipedia.org/wiki/Bombing_of_Tokyo#Results)

20.

The most powerful nuclear device detonated by the USSR had the power of 3000 Hiroshima bombs. A copy of the 26.5 ton bomb is on display in Russia at an exhibition in the Manezh Center near the Kremlin.

Reference: (http://www.bbc.com/news/world-europe-33975032)

21.

The song "Hey There Delilah" by the Plain White T's isn't about a special girl, rather it's about a girl who the lead singer Tom Higgenson met whom he thought was cute.

Reference: (http://youtu.be/jF5lYn3QrKw)

22.

Yale University holds the mysterious "Voynich Manuscript", originating from medieval Europe. It is dotted with illustrations, ranging from astrology to naked women, and written in an unknown language. As yet, nobody has been able to decode it, though it is too systematic to be "random gibberish".

Reference: (http://www.bbc.co.uk/news/science-environment-22975809)

23.

Every year, a town in Sweden builds a large "Yule Goat" made of straw and for most of this goat's history, it has been destroyed by vandals.

Reference: (https://en.wikipedia.org/wiki/G%C3%A4vle_goat)

24.

The "playing dead" defense is actually an involuntary response for an opossum. Stress causes the opossum to go into shock inducing a comatose state lasting anywhere from 40 minutes to 4 hours.

Opossums produce a mucus in this state which smells of decay and often are mistakenly buried alive.

Reference: (http://animals.mom.me/opossums-playing-dead-5274.html)

25.

We typically do not start to think of foods as "too sweet" until our bone growth stops. This means that younger children have virtually no limit to the amount of sugar that they find palatable.

Reference:
(http://www.npr.org/blogs/thesalt/2011/09/26/140753048/kids-sugar-cravings-might-be-biological)

26.

Kurt Cobain spray painted "God Is Gay" on the back of pickup trucks and said he wished he was homosexual, just to "piss off homophobes".

Reference: (http://www.thatericalper.com/2014/04/06/was-kurt-cobain-once-arrested-for-spraypainting-god-is-gay-on-trucks-not-exactly/)

27.

In 1917, the U.S. War Industries Board asked women to stop buying corsets to free up metal for war production. This was said to have saved some 28,000 tons of metal, which was enough to build two battleships.

Reference:
(http://www.pbs.org/wgbh/theymadeamerica/whomade/rosenthal_hi.html)

28.

The USA has been ranked the 2nd most generous country in the world in 2015 by the World Giving Index. Canada was 4th and the U.K. was 6th.

Reference: (https://en.wikipedia.org/wiki/World_Giving_Index)

29.

You have a better chance of predicting which political party will win the presidency in every election from now through 2160 than you do of creating a perfect NCAA bracket.

Reference:
(http://www.usatoday.com/story/news/nation/2014/03/16/buffett-quicken-ncaa-bracket-march-madness-billion-dollars/6410185/)

30.

Alicia Esteve Head is a woman who claimed to have survived the 9/11 attacks and eventually became president of the World Trade Center Survivors' Network before it was revealed in 2007 that she was a fraud and was actually in Spain during the attacks.

Reference: (http://en.wikipedia.org/wiki/Alicia_Esteve_Head)

31.

Influenza is named for the Italian word for "influence". People initially believed that the effects of the flu were a result of the body being "influenced" by astrological changes.

Reference: (https://en.wikipedia.org/wiki/Influenza)

32.

In 1925, The New York Times declared that crossword puzzles weren't going to catch on and that people would get bored of doing them on a weekly basis.

Reference: (http://literarydevices.net/13-thought-provoking-examples-of-irony-in-history/)

33.

People in the Chernobyl clean up team experienced rapid tanning of their skin from exposure to the radiation known as a "nuclear tan".

Reference:(https://en.wikipedia.org/wiki/Individual_involvement_in_the_Chernobyl_disaster#Alexander_Yuvchenko)

34.

In the comic book that The Mask was based on, Stanley Ipkiss was a violent killer.

Reference: (http://channelawesome.com/was-the-mask-supposed-to-be-gory/)

35.

The original "Price Is Right" gave a contestant a real elephant as a gag prize, and planned later to give the winner $4,000 instead. The winner complained and demanded an elephant as promised. The show finally conceded and delivered it to the contestant's home in Texas.

Reference:(http://en.wikipedia.org/wiki/The_Price_Is_Right_%2819 56_U.S._game_show%29#Bloopers)

36.

Sir Godfrey Hounsfield, the Nobel Prize-winning inventor of the CT scanner, funded his first prototype with the EMI record company's profits from the Beatles.

Reference: (http://pubs.rsna.org/doi/full/10.1148/radiol.2343042584)

37.

IKEA hosted a sleepover at their store in England. 100 winners were selected from the 100,000 people that signed up. They had to be over 25 and needed to follow a strict dress code which was pajamas-only.

Reference: (http://adage.com/article/global-news/ikea-u-k-hosts-sleepover-store-100-facebook-fans/231733/)

38.

The history of Australian Aborigines goes back over 70,000 years. An estimated 1.6 billion Aborigines were cumulatively born on the continent before the arrival of Europeans.

Reference:(https://en.wikipedia.org/wiki/History_of_Indigenous_Australians#Before_British_arrival)

39.

A Russian mathematician solved a 100 year old math problem. He declined the Fields Medal, $1 million in awards, and later retired from math because he hated the recognition that the math community gives to people who prove things.

Reference:(https://en.wikipedia.org/wiki/Grigori_Perelman#The_Fields_Medal_and_Millennium_Prize)

40.

A man carved a 360 foot long, 25 foot high, and 30 foot wide path through a hill using only hand tools. This took him 22 years to complete.

Reference: (https://en.wikipedia.org/wiki/Dashrath_Manjhi)

41.

There is an island within the Bay of Bengal that has been isolated from the outside world for the past 65,000 years.

Reference: (https://www.youtube.com/watch?v=f8kV495HQRw)

42.

After a 1610 war with the Kurds, Iran deported many Kurds to the areas of Iran near the Turkmen border in order to weaken and divide them. Their descendants are still alive in these areas today, 400 years later.

Reference: (https://en.wikipedia.org/wiki/Kurds_of_Khorasan)

43.

Stockholm, Sweden tested a "Speed Camera Lottery" where speed limit-abiding drivers were automatically entered into a drawing to win a prize pool funded out of fines paid by speeders.

Reference: (http://www.gamification.co/2013/04/25/gamification-breakdown-of-the-speed-camera-lottery/)

44.

Goofy stance comes from the 1937 Disney animation Hawaiian Holiday where Goofy's most successful attempt at surfing was with his right foot forward.

Reference:
(https://www.youtube.com/watch?v=SdIaEQCUVbk&feature=youtu.be)

45.

The Sun beams that shine through gaps in the clouds are actually called Crepuscular rays.

Reference: (http://www.atoptics.co.uk/atoptics/ray1.htm)

46.

National Doughnut Day, in the United States, is an actual patriotic holiday.

Reference: (https://en.wikipedia.org/wiki/National_Doughnut_Day)

47.

The song "Come Together" by the Beatles was originally created as a campaign song for Timothy Leary when he ran against Ronald Reagan to become the governor of California.

Reference: (http://www.songfacts.com/detail.php?id=191)

48.

In "Back to the Future", they were first thinking of using refrigerators as time machines, and not the DeLorean.

Reference:
(https://en.wikipedia.org/wiki/Back_to_the_Future#Development)

49.

Ricky "The Dragon" Steamboat wrestled by that name because it matched his good guy character better than his real name, which was Rick Blood.

Reference:(https://en.wikipedia.org/wiki/Ricky_Steamboat#Championship_Wrestling_from_Florida_.281976.E2.80.931977.29)

50.

In World War II, British soldiers got a ration of three sheets of toilet paper a day. The Americans got 22.

Reference: (http://books.google.co.uk/books?id=jq8pm--mAuwC&lpg=PA288&ots=etQdS1CRVK&dq=TOILET%20PAPER%20WWII%20SOLDIERS%203%20SHEETS&pg=PA288#v=onepage&q&f=false)

51.

Tom Brady was drafted in the 18th round of the 1995 MLB draft by the Montreal Expos.

Reference:(https://en.wikipedia.org/w/index.php?title=Tom_Brady&
mobileaction=toggle_view_desktop#Early_life)

52.

Hurricane Katrina may be responsible for the recent wave of dystopian fiction, with the chaotic image of the storm and its aftermath kick starting a revival of the genre.

Reference: (http://flavorwire.com/512820/how-hurricane-katrina-gave-rise-to-a1868-flood-of-dystopian-fiction)

53.

Nike lost Stephen Curry to UnderArmour because they thought he did not have a super hero look. Now he is worth $14 billion dollars to UnderArmour.

Reference: (http://espn.go.com/nba/story/_/id/15047018/how-nike-lost-stephen-curry-armour)

54.

The castle in Disney's Parks is actually called Cinderella Castle, not Cinderella's Castle.

Reference: (https://en.wikipedia.org/wiki/Cinderella_Castle)

55.

For nearly a century, the French have prohibited entry into an area of more than 460 square miles because there is an almost impossible amount of ammunition and dead bodies to recover from the battlefields of World War I. The area is called "Zone Rouge", and much of it is still off limits.

Reference: (https://en.wikipedia.org/wiki/Zone_rouge)

56.

Mormons are discouraged from getting tattoos.

Reference: (https://www.lds.org/topics/tattooing?lang=eng)

57.

The fear of the number 666 has a name; hexakosioihexekontahexaphobia.

Reference:
(https://en.wikipedia.org/wiki/Number_of_the_Beast#Fear_and_superstition)

58.

The Temple of Artemis in Ephesus was burned down in 356 BC by a single man who wanted to be famous. The Ephesians condemned him to death and to have his name forgotten, but a writer still passed it down to posterity.

Reference:
(https://en.wikipedia.org/wiki/Temple_of_Artemis#Destruction)

59.

Around 10,000 to 30,000 people each year worked to build St. Petersburg as Russia's new capital for Peter the Great between 1703 and 1725, resulting in about 100,000 deaths. It's considered to be the single major engineering project of the 18th century.

Reference: (http://www.spacesyntax.net/symposia-archive/SSS4/fullpapers/17Knoespelpaper.pdf)

60.

Reintroducing wolves to Yellowstone changed the entire geography of the park: as elk were displaced, saplings that would have been eaten by elk were spared, riverbank erosion was brought under control, and streams and rivers shifted their courses.

Reference: (http://blog.ted.com/2013/09/09/a-walk-on-the-wild-side-7-fascinating-experiments-in-rewilding/)

61.

Ziggy Marley wrote a graphic novel called "Marijuanaman".

Reference: (http://ziggymarley.com/marijuanaman/)

62.

Living near coal-fired power stations exposes people to higher radiation doses than living near nuclear plants.

Reference:
(http://www.inference.phy.cam.ac.uk/withouthotair/c24/page_168.shtml?1)

63.

Ryan Gosling was fired from The Lovely Bones because he was too fat.

Reference: (http://www.hollywoodreporter.com/news/ryan-gosling-peter-jackson-fired-55303)

64.

Only one ship has ever been sunk by a nuclear-powered submarine during military operations.

Reference:
(https://en.wikipedia.org/wiki/ARA_General_Belgrano?repost)

65.

Despite being featured in both "Clash of the Titans" movies, the Kraken is from Norse mythology and not from Greek mythology.

Reference: (https://en.wikipedia.org/wiki/Kraken)

66.

A study done by the Proceedings of the National Academy of Sciences of the United States showed that 1 in 25 prisoner or 4.1% on death row are innocent.

Reference: (http://www.pnas.org/content/111/20/7230)

67.

Musician, Melody Gardot, was left with severe head injuries after an accident at 18. While bedridden, she was encouraged to write music as therapy, even having to relearn to hum due to the extent of her injuries. She has since been nominated for a Grammy and advocates music therapy.

Reference:
(https://en.wikipedia.org/wiki/Melody_Gardot#Accident_and_therapy)

68.

At the 1936 Olympics, Germany released 25,000 pigeons, then fired a canon, resulting in the birds being startled while flying over the crowd.

Reference:
(https://en.wikipedia.org/wiki/1936_Summer_Olympics#Opening_ceremony)

69.

Scatman John had a stutter.

Reference: (https://www.youtube.com/watch?v=K1joxLyd-HA&feature=youtu.be)

70.

Milk isn't good for cats. In fact, the majority of cats are lactose intolerant.

Reference: (http://www.m.webmd.com/a-to-z-guides/cats-and-dairy-get-the-facts)

71.

Before scientists were able to genetically engineer bacteria to produce human insulin, those afflicted with insulin dependent diabetes often used insulin from pigs.

Reference: (http://www.med.uni-giessen.de/itr/history/inshist.html)

72.

In 1978, a man with a shotgun held a Melbourne café hostage until his mother turned up in her night gown and hit him over the head with her handbag. He gave himself up soon after.

Reference: (http://www.theage.com.au/victoria/trotter-v-chopper-day-of-judgment-20121130-2am3m.html)

73.

The Rub' al Khali of the Arabian Peninsula is the largest sand desert in the world; it has an average day temperature of 47 °C, 117 °F, and sand dunes as tall as 250 meters, 820 feet. The Eiffel Tower, for comparison, is 300 meters.

Reference: (https://en.wikipedia.org/wiki/Rub%27_al_Khali)

74.

In 1839, Great Britain declared war on China after its government attempted to cut off the import of opium from the British because too many Chinese people were addicted to the drug.

Reference: (https://en.wikipedia.org/wiki/First_Opium_War)

75.

In Chicago, in 1918, one hundred waiters were taken into custody for poisoning the drinks of people who tipped them poorly.

Reference:(http://en.wikipedia.org/wiki/Mickey_Finn_%28drugs%29#Chicago_restaurant_poisonings)

76.

Pay toilets are virtually unknown in America thanks to a nineteen year-old.

Reference:
(https://en.wikipedia.org/wiki/Committee_to_End_Pay_Toilets_in_America)

77.

The Soviet Navy trained dolphins to kill and then sold them to Iran.

Reference: (https://en.wikipedia.org/wiki/Military_dolphin)

78.

"Accidental incest" is so common in Iceland that a large number of young people use an app to check if it is safe to go home with a stranger, since they may be related.

Reference: (http://www.wired.co.uk/article/iceland-incest-app)

79.

Star Trek writers would write "tech the tech to the warp drive" and let the science consultants figure out the details later.

Reference:
(http://www.blastr.com/2009/10/ron_moore_calls_star_trek.php)

80.

Mick Jagger's singing was criticized for sounding too "posh" until he bit a part of his tongue off playing basketball.

Reference: (http://www.scienceofrock.com/the-other-famous-rolling-stones-tongue)

81.

The Secret Service Museum, a one room museum run by the Secret Service, visiting requires invitation and an agent to escort you. It contains counterfeits, armored car parts, and 9/11 artifacts. It's located in Washington, DC.

Reference: (http://www.c-span.org/video/?296689-1/secret-service-museum)

82.

Bret McKenzie, from Flight of the Concords, played Figwit, that famous elf in the background in Lord of the Rings.

Reference: (https://en.wikipedia.org/wiki/Figwit)

83.

No one knows the etymology of the word "condom"; theories include Latin words condon, which means "receptacle", condamina, which means "house", and cumdum which means "scabbard" or "case".

Reference:
(https://en.wikipedia.org/wiki/History_of_condoms#Etymology_and_other_terms)

84.

There's a Canadian company called C-Fer Technologies that allows pipeline operators and companies developing leak-sensing technologies to test pipes in real conditions with 24 foot length of pipe riddled with adjustable leak ports and embedded in a tank of dirt.

Reference: (http://www.wired.com/2014/11/c-fer-technologies/)

85.

Vin Diesel helped produced and financed Riddick (2013) and even put up his house as collateral to get it made. "If we didn't finish the film, I would be homeless".

Reference: (https://gma.yahoo.com/blogs/abc-blogs/vin-diesel-had-leverage-house-riddick-103558491--abc-news-celebrities.html)

86.

A baby girl can express milk from her nipples and have a period within 2 to 3 days of being born.

Reference: (http://www.parents.com/baby/care/newborn/whats-normal-for-your-newborn/)

87.

Richard Nixon's name in American Sign Language is the sign for "LIE" with the N handshape.

Reference:
(http://www.handspeak.com/word/search/index.php?id=6617)

88.

The third most popular male baby name in Iceland is Guðmundur.

Reference: (http://clickbabynames.com/35803/top-100-baby-names-in-iceland)

89.

The RMS Olympic received a distress call from its sister ship, the Titanic. On its way to the scene, another ship radioed in to not come pick up any survivors, as it would cause panic among the already traumatized survivors to have to be put on a ship that's virtually a mirror image of the Titanic.

Reference:
(https://en.wikipedia.org/wiki/RMS_Olympic#Titanic_disaster)

90.

Crows display an understanding of water displacement and can use this to solve puzzles.

Reference:
(https://www.youtube.com/watch?v=ZerUbHmuY04&feature=youtu.be)

91.

The oldest song in the world was written over 3,300 years ago in the 14th Century BCE by Sumerians in the city of Ugarit. Discovered on cuneiform tablets in the 1950s, it changed beliefs in musicology concerning harmonization and scales, pushing them back by 600 years. It is still performed live.

Reference: (http://ledgernote.com/blog/culture/first-song-ever-written/)

92.

American bison's were hunted with the intention of destroying the food source of the natives.

Reference: (https://en.wikipedia.org/wiki/Bison_hunting)

93.

Christopher Poole, the creator of controversial website 4chan, began working for Google in 2016.

Reference: (https://en.wikipedia.org/wiki/Christopher_Poole)

94.

The default Windows 10 wallpaper isn't a CGI image, it's a practical effect.

Reference: (https://www.youtube.com/watch?v=hL8BBOwupcI)

95.

During World War II, MLB player, Moe Berg, attended a lecture by physicist Heisenberg with a gun. Berg planned to kill Heisenberg should he reveal that the Nazis were close to completing the bomb. No reveal was made and, unclear on the bomb's status, Berg let Heisenberg live, later calling the event his own, "Uncertainty Principle."

Reference:
(https://en.wikipedia.org/wiki/Werner_Heisenberg#World_War_II)

96.

38% of people in Vietnam have the last name Nguyen.

Reference:
(https://en.wikipedia.org/wiki/Vietnamese_name#Family_name)

97.

Stir frying wasn't a common cooking technique in the home in China until the 20th century, when cooking oil and fuel became more affordable.

Reference: (https://en.wikipedia.org/wiki/Stir_frying)

98.

John Wayne smoked 6 packs of cigarettes a day.

Reference:
(https://en.wikipedia.org/wiki/The_Conqueror_(film)#Cancer_contro versy)

99.

Mad Men paid $250,000 for the master recording of "Tomorrow Never Knows" by The Beatles. They played it for just two minutes during a Season 5 episode.

Reference: (http://www.businessinsider.com/mad-men-paid-250k-to-use-beatles-song-2014-4)

100.

The highest flying bird is the Rüppell's vulture and one was found to be ingested by a jet at 37,000 feet.

Reference:
(https://en.wikipedia.org/wiki/R%C3%BCppell%27s_vulture)

101.

The U.K. Army wanted to use chickens to keep a nuclear landmine warm.

Reference: (http://news.bbc.co.uk/2/hi/uk_news/3588465.stm)

102.

Male chicks hatched in an egg hatchery on industrial farms are ground up alive because they are unable to lay eggs.

Reference: (https://www.youtube.com/watch?v=JJ--faib7to)

103.

James Audubon, painter and founder of the conservationist Audubon society, killed every bird he painted.

Reference:
(https://en.wikipedia.org/wiki/John_James_Audubon#Art_and_methods)

104.

George Clooney's private satellites have captured piles of bodies and mass graves in Sudan.

Reference: (http://nation.time.com/2011/07/14/clooneys-satellites-capture-piles-of-bodies-mass-graves-in-sudan/)

105.

The oldest person ever recorded was 122 years old and smoked cigarettes for 96 years. She also ate 2 pounds of chocolate every week.

Reference: (https://en.wikipedia.org/wiki/Jeanne_Calment)

106.

In 1965, NASA tested out the effects of being in a vacuum on dogs which resulted in, "simultaneous defecation, projectile vomiting and urination. They suffered massive seizures. Their tongues were often coated in ice and the dogs swelled to resemble an inflated goatskin bag."

Reference: (http://www.scientificamerican.com/article/survival-in-space-unprotected-possible)

107.

The reason a Metroid game was never created for the Nintendo 64 was because the co-creator of Metroid, Yoshio Sakamoto, couldn't figure out how to use the Nintendo 64 controller.

Reference: (http://www.themarysue.com/metroid-n64-canceled/)

108.

The Puckle gun was an early machine gun that was invented in 1717.

Reference: (https://en.wikipedia.org/wiki/Puckle_gun)

109.

North Korea's urban slum area is between 0% and 10%, which is better than South Korea and the majority of South East Asia.

Reference: (https://en.wikipedia.org/wiki/Slum)

110.

Seann William Scott, who played Stifler in the American Pie films, was extremely shy and nervous around women and did not have a girlfriend until he was 30 years old.

Reference: (http://www.imdb.com/name/nm0005405/bio)

111.

A "Batman" is a personal servant of a military leader. In the DC Comics media, Alfred Pennyworth is sometimes referred to as "Batman's Batman".

Reference:
(https://en.wikipedia.org/wiki/Batman_(military)#Fiction)

112.

During her husband's third term as president from 1973 to 1974, Isabel Peron served as both Vice President and First Lady. When her husband died, she became President of Argentina and thus became the first female president of any country in the world.

Reference:
(https://en.wikipedia.org/wiki/Isabel_Mart%C3%ADnez_de_Per%C3%B3n)

113.

Family Guy faced a boycott from a group called ProudSponsorsUSA because of the offensive nature of the show. It turned out to be just Richardson Schell, who was the headmaster of MacFarlane's High

School. He was actually upset because of the use of the name Griffin, the name of Schell's assistant.

Reference: (http://www.nytimes.com/1999/07/01/arts/irate-headmaster-irreverent-alumnus-the-family-guy-saga.html)

114.

Netflix streamed 1,348 hours of content each second in 2015, for a total of 42.5 billion hours in total.

Reference: (http://www.broadbandsearch.net/page/netflix-streaming-in-motion?kd)

115.

After September 11th occurred in the United States, every major U.S. airline that exists today declared bankruptcy.

Reference: (http://bold.global/david-grasso/2015/12/04/airlines-profitability-mediocrity/)

116.

France has no official racial statistics, due to being an "ideally colorblind republicanism".

Reference:(http://www.theroot.com/articles/world/2012/05/france_race_statistics_there_arent_any_and_thats_the_problem/)

117.

Mormon underwear, or Temple garment, is a type of underwear worn by adherents of the Latter Day Saint movement throughout their lives.

Reference: (https://en.wikipedia.org/wiki/Temple_garment)

118.

Adam in Genesis is not actually named Adam, Adam is simply the Hebrew word for "man."

Reference:
(https://www.biblegateway.com/passage/?search=Genesis%202&version=NIV)

119.

Jack Kerouac wrote in Esquire magazine that his quest to find the ideal bar ended in Butte, Montana, at the M&M Bar, when he visited the infamous town in 1970.

Reference: (http://retracingjackkerouac.com/2014/08/29/m-m-cigar-store-butte-montana/)

120.

Viagra was originally developed for high blood pressure, but volunteers in the clinical trials reported increased erections several days after taking a dose of the drug.

Reference: (http://www.cnn.com/2013/03/27/health/viagra-anniversary-timeline/index.html)

121.

Famous porn star Peter North initially entered the industry doing gay porn under the name Matt Ramsey.

Reference: (https://en.wikipedia.org/wiki/Peter_North_(actor))

122.

Seinfeld's bass intro is actually played on a keyboard, is composed of an audio range that doesn't interfere with Jerry's voice, and was redone every episode to match the pacing of Jerry's monologue.

Reference:
(https://www.youtube.com/watch?v=oVldNNHQWVw&feature=youtu.be&t=16s)

123.

The working title of the movie Hitch starring Will Smith was originally The Last First Kiss.

Reference: (https://en.wikipedia.org/wiki/Hitch_(film))

124.

Deforestation accounts for 10% of greenhouse gas emissions.

Reference: (http://www.redd-monitor.org/2014/02/15/redd-myth-no-1-deforestation-accounts-for-25-of-greenhouse-gas-emissions/)

125.

A Pennsylvania man shot a gun into his neighbor's house while trying to clear the chamber. He stated in court that firing the gun was the only way that he knew to unload it.

Reference: (http://news.yahoo.com/cops-man-fired-neighbors-home-unload-gun-233642863.html)

126.

Blue belly lizards eradicated Lyme disease from the ticks that bite them. This is believed to be the reason why Lyme is less prevalent in California and other western states.

Reference: (http://www.sfgate.com/health/article/Lizards-Slow-Lyme-Disease-in-West-Ticks-bite-3009330.php?forceWeb=1)

127.

A professional gamer by the name "agwawaf" beat Megaman X, X2 and X3 simultaneously with the same controller.

Reference:
(https://www.youtube.com/watch?v=HesqAy0Vf48&feature=youtu.be&t=1m33s)

128.

Fanta was originally created in Nazi Germany when a trade embargo prevented Germany from receiving Coca Cola syrup, so they created a drink with available ingredients instead.

Reference: (https://en.wikipedia.org/wiki/Fanta#History)

129.

The game Keno started in Butte, Montana, by brothers who adapted the game from Chinese gamblers who played it in local bars. It became popular after the brothers brought it to Las Vegas.

Reference: (http://www.butteamerica.com/mm.htm)

130.

Stephen Sondheim wrote a musical based on a creepy short story about people secretly living in a department store.

Reference:
(http://www.npr.org/templates/story/story.php?storyId=130811886)

131.

In 1993, Egyptologists sent a small rover through one of the Air Shafts of the Great Pyramid. The rover came in contact with a stone door with two copper handles attached. To this day, the door has not been opened and now one knows where it leads.

Reference: (https://www.newscientist.com/article/mg21028144.500-first-images-from-great-pyramids-chamber-of-secrets)

132.

Fugazi's Ian MacKaye would still give ticket refunds to people escorted out of the band's shows for being too violent, and kept envelopes containing $5 bills in the tour van for this very purpose.

Reference:
(https://en.wikipedia.org/wiki/Fugazi#Business_practices)

133.

In 2011, a drunk armed Royal Navy sailor opened fire aboard a nuclear submarine, killing one officer and injuring another.

Reference: (https://en.wikipedia.org/wiki/HMS_Astute_(S119))

134.

Orson Scott Card, the author of Ender's Game, helped write the insults from "The Secret of Monkey Island."

Reference:
(https://en.wikipedia.org/wiki/The_Secret_of_Monkey_Island)

135.

Cytokines, proteins that cause inflammation and tell the body to go into "sickness mode" increase in number during depressive episodes. Researchers are beginning to investigate the link between depression and inflammation/allergic reactions in the body.

Reference: (http://www.psychologytoday.com/blog/the-breakthrough-depression-solution/201111/the-brain-fire-inflammation-and-depression)

136.

A third of all North American bird species need urgent conservation action.

Reference: (http://www.stateofthebirds.org/2016/overview/results-summary/)

137.

The founder of American Apparel, Dov Charney, is actually a Canadian.

Reference: (https://en.wikipedia.org/wiki/Dov_Charney)

138.

Vince McMahon's grandfather was business partners with the original owner of the New York Rangers, Tex Rickard.

Reference:
(https://en.wikipedia.org/wiki/Tex_Rickard#Rickard_and_1920s_boxing)

139.

The Big Bang Theory doesn't use a laugh track, and is shot in front of a live studio audience. Tickets are offered for free to any legal adult.

Reference: (http://the-big-bang-theory.com/tickets/)

140.

Doritos are addicting due to two acids which trigger the impulse to eat by increasing saliva flow.

Reference: (http://nypost.com/2013/10/03/why-doritos-are-as-addictive-as-crack/)

141.

There is a study that concludes 45% of jobs will be replaced with automation within the next 20 years.

Reference:
(http://www.oxfordmartin.ox.ac.uk/publications/view/1314)

142.

"Someday My Prince Will Come" was first played in jazz form by a band formed in a concentration camp.

Reference:(https://en.wikipedia.org/wiki/Someday_My_Prince_Will_Come#As_a_jazz_standard)

143.

Ganymede, one of Jupiter's moons, probably contains more water than Earth.

Reference: (http://www.space.com/28807-jupiter-moon-ganymede-salty-ocean.html)

144.

Blind people supplement synthetic melatonin, a hormone that regulates sleep cycles, in order to teach their brains when it's day and night. Without it, they're arguably in a state of perpetual jet lag.

Reference: (https://en.wikipedia.org/wiki/Melatonin)

145.

There are pig rescue organizations that help place and find homes for unwanted, abandoned, abused potbellied pigs, such as those that buyers mistakenly believe will stay as "teacup pigs" forever but end up growing into full sized potbellied pigs.

Reference: (http://www.teacuppig.info/Pig_Sanctuaries.html)

146.

The phrase "crocodile tears" derives from an ancient belief that crocodiles shed tears while consuming their prey.

Reference: (https://en.wikipedia.org/wiki/Crocodile_tears)

147.

19% of high school graduates in the U.S. can't read above a basic level.

Reference: (http://www.statisticbrain.com/number-of-american-adults-who-cant-read/)

148.

Supernatural fans used the hash tag #LuciferIsComing for the 5th season premiere when Lucifer is released, but unaware Twitter users responded with numerous #GodIsHere hash tags, leading both topics to be blocked from Twitter.

Reference:
(https://en.wikipedia.org/wiki/Supernatural_(U.S._TV_series))

149.

There are no specific constitutional qualifications for Supreme Court nominees. There is no age requirement, you don't have to be American born, and no law dictates that a nominee has to be a lawyer.

Reference: (http://thelawdictionary.org/article/qualifications-to-become-a-supreme-court-justice/)

150.

22 years ago, a Stardust Casino employee walked out of the hotel with $500,000 and was never seen again.

Reference: (http://www.casinob.com/casino-blog/las-vegas/the-stardust-casino-heist/)

151.

The expression "spitting image" refers to ejaculation.

Reference: (http://articles.chicagotribune.com/2010-12-22/features/ct-tribu-words-work-spit-20101222_1_splitting-image-linguistics-mirror-images)

152.

To make decaf coffee beans, coffee beans are steamed for 30 minutes, rinsed with dichloromethane or ethyl acetate for about 10 hours then steamed for an additional 10 hours to remove residual solvent.

Reference: (https://en.wikipedia.org/wiki/Decaffeination#Decaffeination_proces ses_for_coffee)

153.

The inspiration for the phrase "coals to Newcastle" was an ancient Greek phrase literally meaning "owls to Athens".

Reference: (http://etymonline.com/index.php?term=coal&allowed_in_frame=0)

154.

Authors J.R.R. Tolkien and C.S. Lewis made a pact to write books on two topics. Lewis would take "space travel," while Tolkien would take "time travel." Lewis completed his "space travel" trilogy, but Tolkien never finished his "time travel" books. Instead, Tolkien wrote "The Lord of the Rings" trilogy.

Reference: (http://www.christianitytoday.com/history/2008/august/j-r-r-tolkien-and-c-s-lewis-legendary-friendship.html)

155.

With an EPA Energy Star rating of 84, the New York Chrysler Building that was built in the 1930s is more energy efficient than the new 7 World Trade Center by 10 points, thanks to its thicker walls and fewer windows that results in a better thermal envelope.

Reference: (http://www.energymanagertoday.com/chrysler-building-more-energy-efficient-than-world-trade-center-087933/)

156.

Janis Joplin and Jimi Hendrix died sixteen days apart.

Reference: (http://www.nydailynews.com/entertainment/music/27-club-famous-musicians-died-age-27-article-1.2501832)

157.

The Spanish dollar remained legal tender in the United States until the Coinage Act of 1857.

Reference: (https://en.wikipedia.org/wiki/Spanish_dollar)

158.

"The Matrix" film makers, the Wachowski brothers, are now the Wachowski sisters.

Reference: (https://www.theguardian.com/film/2016/mar/10/the-matrix-wachowski-siblings-men-rights-activists)

159.

There is a planet that is completely covered in ice, but is constantly on fire. The reason the ice doesn't melt is because the gravity is so strong that it pulls the ice towards it, compressing it in the process.

Reference:
(https://en.wikipedia.org/wiki/Gliese_436_b#Physical_characteristics)

160.

A Harvard Researcher found rolling a pair of dice was as predictive of your future income as your college GPA is.

Reference: (http://www.bakadesuyo.com/2014/09/be-more-successful/)

161.

Gert Postel, a German impostor, worked as a psychiatrist for 15 years and got appointed to a professorship without ever having received training or graduating from high school.

Reference: (https://en.wikipedia.org/wiki/Gert_Postel)

162.

Electronics Corporation Sharp invented the modern mechanical pencil, and even got its name from its "Ever-Ready Sharp" pencil.

Reference: (http://www.vintagepens.com/Eversharp_history.htm)

163.

Animals have certain blood groupings and you can have your pet donate blood to help other animals in need.

Reference: (https://vet.osu.edu/vmc/companion/our-services/animal-blood-bank/faq-blood-donors)

164.

Margaret and H.A. Rey built bicycles from spare parts to escape the Nazis while carrying the manuscript of Curious George with them.

Reference: (http://www.nytimes.com/2005/09/13/books/how-curious-george-escaped-the-nazis.html)

165.

The video game company, SEGA, actually started in the United States before it moved to Japan.

Reference:
(https://en.wikipedia.org/wiki/Sega#Company_origins_.281940.E2.8
0.931982.29)

166.

Research suggests that if a pregnant woman suffers a heart attack, the fetus will donate some of its stem cells to help rebuild the damaged heart tissue.

Reference: (https://www.fightaging.org/archives/2011/11/fetal-stem-cells-can-repair-the-mother-during-pregnancy/)

167.

The Mona Lisa was stolen in 1911, and was missing for 2 years.

Reference:
(http://history1900s.about.com/od/famouscrimesscandals/a/monalisa
.htm)

168.

Some spiders consume pollen, consisting of up to a quarter of their diets.

Reference:
(https://www.sciencedaily.com/releases/2013/12/131218100133.htm
)

169.

Kyle Gass gave Jack Black guitar lessons in exchange for a Jack in the Box.

Reference: (https://en.wikipedia.org/wiki/Tenacious_D)

170.

Fred Tuttle was a Vermont dairy farmer who was also an indie film star of a mockumentary about a dairy farmer running for Senate. Two years later, he ran for real and won the primary.

Reference: (http://www.washingtonpost.com/wp-srv/politics/campaigns/keyraces98/stories/vt090498.htm)

171.

Cryovolcanos, or "Ice Volcanoes", form on cold moons and, instead of magma, they erupt ice and volatile gases. There are several documented within our solar system.

Reference: (https://en.wikipedia.org/wiki/Cryovolcano)

172.

It's more efficient to not allow people to pass you on a crowded escalator, because keeping a lane open for passers reduces the total capacity of the escalator by a third or more.

Reference: (https://www.theguardian.com/uk-news/2016/jan/16/the-tube-at-a-standstill-why-tfl-stopped-people-walking-up-the-escalators)

173.

Lake Constance is the only area in Europe where no borders exist, because there is no legally binding agreement as to where the borders lie between Switzerland, Germany and Austria.

Reference:
(https://en.wikipedia.org/wiki/Lake_Constance#International_borders)

174.

The look for Mad Magazine's famous mascot, Alfred E. Neuman, was based on 19th century anti-Irish propaganda.

Reference: (http://www.toledoblade.com/Art/2008/01/20/Mad-for-Alfred-A-new-exhibit-shows-Mad-magazine-s-poster-boy-has-a-shadowy-past.html)

175.

Albert Einstein had a silk bathrobe that he would "accidentally" let open in front of certain woman. He would then make a move based on their reaction.

Reference: (http://www.biography.com/people/albert-einstein-9285408/videos/albert-einstein-full-episode-2073090093)

176.

Cats have a parasite called Toxoplasma gondii that they pass to rats which alters the behavior of the rats to make them easier prey for the cats.

Reference: (https://schizophreniabulletin.oxfordjournals.org/content/33/3/752.full)

177.

AIDS was once known as the "4H Disease", as it was believed to affect heroin addicts, homosexuals, hemophiliacs, and Haitians only.

Reference: (https://en.wikipedia.org/wiki/HIV/AIDS#Discovery)

178.

Candle flames contain millions of tiny diamonds, as they contain all four known forms of carbon.

Reference: (http://phys.org/news/2011-08-candle-flames-millions-tiny-diamonds.html)

179.

The Landkreuzer P. 1000 Ratte is the biggest tank that Hitler approved before its bigger brother was imagined.

Reference:
(https://en.wikipedia.org/wiki/Landkreuzer_P._1000_Ratte)

180.

A giant mansion, known as the Penmore Castle, is being built as an apocalypse safe house in rural Missouri.

Reference: (http://www.ozarksfirst.com/story/d/story/what-is-going-on-inside-pensmore-castle/33815/CTwBv4-e4kG-F-hmFe0-nQ)

181.

A study in the Journal of Sex Research showed that porn viewers seem to think more highly of women than those who do not watch porn.

Reference: (http://www.psypost.org/2016/03/porn-viewers-think-highly-women-41404)

182.

One of Gandhi's biggest influences was Leo Tolstoy.

Reference: (http://www.asthabharati.org/Dia_Oct%20010/y.p..htm)

183.

The Rainbow Flag was designed by San Francisco artist Gilbert Baker in 1978; the design has undergone several revisions to first remove then to re-add colors due to widely available fabrics.

Reference:
(https://en.wikipedia.org/wiki/Rainbow_flag_(LGBT_movement))

184.

West Virginia is the only state in the union to have experienced a decline in population from 2010 to 2015.

Reference:
(https://en.wikipedia.org/wiki/List_of_U.S._states_by_population_growth_rate)

185.

A man loved his goldfish so much that he paid almost $500 for a lifesaving surgery to remove its constipation.

Reference: (http://www.mirror.co.uk/news/weird-news/man-loves-constipated-goldfish-much-4904409)

186.

Feynman didn't believe in washing your hands after urinating.

Reference: (https://www.youtube.com/watch?v=rnMsgxIIQEE)

187.

There's a river called River Suck, connected to the River Shannon, in Ireland.

Reference: (https://en.wikipedia.org/wiki/River_Suck)

188.

Limp Bizkit was almost called Gimp Disco and Bitch Piglet.

Reference: (http://www.frusanes.com/2015/03/how-these-famous-music-bands-got-their.html)

189.

Most pool tables use one of two methods to separate the cue ball from the rest of the balls in return. Some use a larger cue ball, but most use metal in the ball and magnets to send it down a different track.

Reference: (http://electronics.howstuffworks.com/question495.htm)

190.

The show, MythBusters, confirmed the myth that a scuba diver can wear a tuxedo underneath his drysuit, go underwater, resurface, strip off his scuba gear, and be able to present the tuxedo at a yacht party in the harbor as James Bond did in the movie, "Goldfinger."

Reference: (http://www.discovery.com/tv-shows/mythbusters/mythbusters-database/scuba-dive-in-a-tux/)

191.

There's a psychological disorder where people think they're cows. It' called boanthropy.

Reference: (https://en.wikipedia.org/wiki/Boanthropy)

192.

The singer Phil Collins is an Alamo history buff, Alamo artifact collector and "honorary Texan".

Reference: (http://www.history.com/news/phil-collins-has-always-remembered-the-alamo)

193.

A song in the original Pokémon games contained sounds that were outside the adult hearing range, but within the child hearing range, which caused many conspiracy theories and online myths.

Reference:
(http://bulbapedia.bulbagarden.net/wiki/Lavender_Town#Trivia)

194.

The word "gross", meaning "disgusting", is a slang word that originated in the 1950s.

Reference:
(http://www.etymonline.com/index.php?allowed_in_frame=0&searc
h=gross)

195.

The 1987 movie, "The Running Man," starred two future governors; Arnold Schwarzenegger, who was the Governor of California and Jesse Venture, who was the Governor of Minnesota.

Reference: (http://www.imdb.com/title/tt0093894/)

196.

A large pile of hollowed-out snow is called a "quinzhee". This is in contrast to an "igloo", which is made from blocks of hard snow.

Reference: (https://en.wikipedia.org/wiki/Quinzhee)

197.

Sara Watkins, bluegrass musician of Nickel Creek fame, had her debut solo album produced by John Paul Jones, formerly of Led Zeppelin.

Reference: (https://en.wikipedia.org/wiki/Sara_Watkins_(album))

198.

The warrior women mentioned in the Iliad, the Amazons, do not come from South America. Rather, the river was named by Spanish explorers who encountered fierce women that reminded them of the Amazons from the Iliad.

Reference: (https://en.wikipedia.org/wiki/Amazons)

199.

Nectar robbing is removing nectar from a flowering plant by piercing a hole on the side of the flower, rather than entering the natural opening.

Reference: (https://en.wikipedia.org/wiki/Nectar_robbing)

200.

You would get a larger dose of radiation from eating a bag of potato chips every day than you would if you lived next to a nuclear power plant.

Reference: (http://www.forbes.com/sites/jamesconca/2013/04/01/do-nuclear-power-plants-cause-cancer/)

201.

There was an alternate universe Superman comic, in which he lands in Russia as a baby, instead of in the USA, and Superman becomes Russia's greatest weapon.

Reference: (http://comicvine.gamespot.com/red-son-superman/4005-70538/)

202.

Johnny Rico from Starship Troopers was a Filipino man in the 1959 novel of the same name.

Reference: (https://en.wikipedia.org/wiki/Juan_Rico)

203.

Joaquin Phoenix's family was part of a controversial cult "Children of God". Joaquin's brother, River Phoenix, who died in 1993 of a drug overdose on Halloween Night, claimed to have lost his virginity there at 4 years old.

Reference: (https://en.wikipedia.org/wiki/River_Phoenix)

204.

Babies shouldn't drink water.

Reference: (http://www.who.int/features/qa/breastfeeding/en/)

205.

Carvings of naked women with stretched out vaginas were being commonly placed on churches in Ireland and Britain during the Middle Ages.

Reference: (http://en.wikipedia.org/wiki/Sheela_na_gig)

206.

In 2009, in New York City, a drunk man stiffed a cab driver, ran away from him into a random apartment building where security chased him. He ran up to the 35th floor and accidentally fell to his death in the building's trash compactor.

Reference:
(http://gothamist.com/2009/04/13/man_stiffs_cabbie_falls_to_death_in.php)

207.

President Ronald Reagan really liked Jelly Belly jelly beans.

Reference: (https://www.jellybelly.com/fun-facts)

208.

Birds are dinosaurs; they are considered "avian dinosaurs" and have been around for 100 million years, thus making them the last living dinosaurs on Earth.

Reference: (https://en.wikipedia.org/wiki/Bird)

209.

There exists a math competition with a $175,000 cash prize for the first three students and a whole week in a 5 star hotel on an exotic island for 30 teachers.

Reference: (http://grandsentinel.com/)

210.

Even though Google's self-driving cars have logged over 700,000 miles, they have yet to overcome the navigational hurdles of snow, heavy rain, open parking lots, multilevel parking garages, construction zones, and when the sun is directly behind a traffic light.

Reference: (http://www.digitaltrends.com/cars/googles-self-driving-car-far-ready-cant-drive-rain-snow-parking-lots/)

211.

In 1962, President Kennedy invited 49 Nobel Laureates for dinner at the White House. Kennedy remarked, "I think this is the most extraordinary collection of talent, of human knowledge, that has ever been gathered at the White House, with the possible exception of when Thomas Jefferson dined alone."

Reference: (http://www.presidency.ucsb.edu/ws/?pid=8623)

212.

Urinating in the shower can save up to 2,500 liters of water per year, per person.

Reference: (http://designtoimprovelife.dk/waterurinepee/)

213.

Shaquille O'Neal has a doctorate in education and wrote his thesis on humor in the workplace.

Reference:
(http://www.nytimes.com/2012/05/06/sports/basketball/shaquille-oneal-earns-his-doctorate-in-education.html?_r=0)

214.

A woman pled guilty to forging prescriptions and gave the judge a doctor's note. This also turned out to be forged.

Reference:
(http://www.sanluisobispo.com/news/local/article39147714.html)

215.

Romans kept track of the years by naming them after two consuls that year; for example, the consulship of Vinicius and Haterius. When Julius Caesar essentially ruled alone during his "co-consulship" with Bibulus, Romans joked by referring to that year as the consulship of Julius and Caesar.

Reference: (http://www.vroma.org/~bmcmanus/caesar.html)

216.

Standard Oil, between 1943 and 1956, had photographers document the benefits of oil on everyday life and these photos offer the largest representation of American life from this time period.

Reference:
(http://digital.library.louisville.edu/cdm/landingpage/collection/sonj/
)

217.

Volkswagen Group, that has the largest market share in Europe, sells passenger cars, motorcycles and commercial vehicles under the marques: Audi, Bentley, Bugatti, Lamborghini, Porsche, SEAT, Škoda, Volkswagen, Ducati, MAN, Scania, Neoplan and Volkswagen Commercial Vehicles.

Reference: (https://en.wikipedia.org/wiki/Volkswagen_Group)

218.

NOAA announced that it was to start using lowercase letters in forecasts by saying "NOAA'S NATIONAL WEATHER SERVICE FORECASTS WILL STOP YELLING AT YOU".

Reference: (http://www.noaa.gov/national-weather-service-will-stop-using-all-caps-its-forecasts)

219.

Biotech firm Pambient has managed to 3D print fake rhino horns that are genetically identical knock offs. The company plans to flood the Chinese rhino horn market at one-eighth of the price of the original, undercutting the price poachers can get and forcing them out eventually.

Reference: (http://news.nationalgeographic.com/2015/12/151203-pembient-synthetic-rhino-horn-vietnam-poaching/)

220.

The United States is the two time defending Olympic Gold Medalist in Rugby.

Reference: (http://olympictalk.nbcsports.com/2015/06/14/usa-rugby-qualifies-rio-olympics-2016/)

221.

HMS Dreadnought was the only battleship ever to sink a submarine, and that for a ship designed for naval warfare, this was her only major achievement.

Reference:
(https://en.wikipedia.org/wiki/HMS_Dreadnought_(1906)#Service_record)

222.

The Pledge of Allegiance in America, before 1942, was recited while extending the arm straight forward, angling slightly upward with fingers pointing directly ahead.

Reference: (http://www.cnn.com/2013/12/22/opinion/greene-pledge-of-allegiance-salute/)

223.

There exists a massive abandoned supercollider in Texas.

Reference: (http://sometimes-interesting.com/2012/01/31/worlds-largest-super-collider-abandoned/#more-2259)

224.

There is a legend that Spanish sounds strange because one of its Kings lisped and made everyone else in the country do it as well.

Reference: (https://en.wikipedia.org/wiki/Phonological_history_of_Spanish_coronal_fricatives)

225.

For many years, "computer" was a job title for a person who did math problems all day long.

Reference: (http://en.wikipedia.org/wiki/Human_computer)

226.

There is a length of border between USA and Canada that is marked by deforestation.

Reference: (https://www.youtube.com/watch?v=qMkYllA7mgw)

227.

Inanimate objects can be sued; for example, "United States v. Approximately 64,695 Pounds of Shark Fins."

Reference: (https://en.wikipedia.org/wiki/In_rem_jurisdiction?2)

228.

Urinary tract infections arising after sex are called "Honeymoon Cystitis".

Reference:
(https://en.wikipedia.org/wiki/Urinary_tract_infection#Sex)

229.

A children's toy company named Goliath Games made a board game where the objective of the game is to collect as much feces as possible from a toy dog. They also made games such as "Who Tooted?" and "Gooey Louie."

Reference: (https://www.youtube.com/watch?v=JDyOD1C67J0)

230.

Excessive exposure to the chemical TBT has caused female snails in Australia to grow penises on their heads.

Reference: (http://www.wired.co.uk/news/archive/2010-09/15/chemical-causes-female-snails-to-grow-penises-on-their-heads-)

231.

The Carlton Dance was inspired by the dance that Courteney Cox does in the Bruce Springsteen music video "Dancing in the Dark".

Reference: (http://freshprince.wikia.com/wiki/Carlton_Dance)

232.

The Eurasian water shrew has venomous saliva, making it one of the few venomous mammals, although it is not able to puncture the skin of large animals such as humans.

Reference: (https://en.wikipedia.org/wiki/Eurasian_water_shrew)

233.

"ALFA", later Alfa Romeo, was an acronym for "Anonima Lombarda Fabbrica Automobili," founded 1910.

Reference: (https://en.wikipedia.org/wiki/Alfa_Romeo)

234.

There are drones that can build bridges autonomously.

Reference: (https://www.youtube.com/watch?v=kueC7ZnBXz8)

235.

Enterprising Kenyans pretended to be Somali pirates and gave fake interviews to foreign journalists for cash.

Reference: (http://blog.priceonomics.com/post/47213779581/now-hiring-fake-somali-pirates)

236.

Kanye West was caught torrenting editing software from The Pirate Bay.

Reference:
(http://www.popularmechanics.com/culture/music/a19714/kanye-busted-torrenting-editing-software-from-the-pirate-bay/)

237.

From the time that it was discovered to the time that it was de-classified as a planet, Pluto has not made a full rotation around the Sun.

Reference: (https://simple.wikipedia.org/wiki/Pluto)

238.

Upon arrival in Tokyo for Wings' highly anticipated 1980 sold out tour, Paul McCartney was arrested at the airport after a search of his luggage revealed 219 grams of marijuana. The tour was cancelled and McCartney spent nine days in jail.

Reference:
(https://en.wikipedia.org/wiki/McCartney_II#Background)

239.

When Dr. Dre was in N.W.A., he rapped about how he didn't smoke marijuana because it was known to cause brain damage. 4 year later, he released "The Chronic."

Reference: (https://www.youtube.com/watch?v=u31FO_4d9TY)

240.

A New Zealand man won the French Scrabble Championship by memorizing the French Scrabble Dictionary in 9 weeks.

Reference:
(http://www.theguardian.com/lifeandstyle/2015/jul/21/new-french-scrabble-champion-nigel-richards-doesnt-speak-french)

241.

Adam Rainer was the only man known to have been both a dwarf and a giant. At the age of 21, he measured only 118 centimeters tall, but by the end of his life he was the tallest man in Austria at 234 centimeters.

Reference: (https://www.damninteresting.com/the-man-who-was-a-dwarf-and-a-giant/)

242.

Dwayne "The Rock" Johnson eats up to 10 pounds of food per day to maintain his physique.

Reference: (http://fivethirtyeight.com/datalab/dwayne-the-rock-johnson-eats-about-821-pounds-of-cod-per-year/)

243.

The movie "Zootopia" is actually called "Zootropolis" in the U.K. as Zootopia is the name of an actual zoo.

Reference: (https://en.wikipedia.org/wiki/Zootopia)

244.

Daredevil's black ninja outfit originated in a television movie where Matt Murdock defends the Hulk. This likely later inspired the Frank Miller's "The Man Without Fear," which introduced a similar suit into the comics.

Reference:
(https://en.wikipedia.org/wiki/The_Trial_of_the_Incredible_Hulk)

245.

There   are
80,658,175,170,943,878,571,660,636,856,403,766,975,289,505,440, 883,277,824,
000,000,000,000,000 different ways to shuffle a deck of cards.

Reference: (http://www.wolframalpha.com/input/?i=52%21)

246.

The elephant-headed Hindu god Ganesha has an elephant head because after he was decapitated by demons that was the first replacement that could be found.

Reference: (http://www.ancient.eu/Ganesha/)

247.

One raspberry contains one calorie.

Reference: (http://www.calorieking.com/foods/calories-in-fresh-fruits-raspberries-raw_f-ZmlkPTYzNjAz.html)

248.

"V for Vendetta" was broadcast in China without any censorship, surprising many viewers.

Reference:
(https://en.wikipedia.org/wiki/V_for_Vendetta_(film)#Political)

249.

Your eyes "turn off" when they undergo rapid motions to assess your field of vision, leaving you momentarily blind.

Reference:
(http://www.scholarpedia.org/article/Human_saccadic_eye_movements)

250.

The only known recording of Hitler's voice where he is not giving a speech was from a private conversation between him and the Finnish leader Mannerheim. The private conversation was recorded in secrecy by a sound engineer in 1942.

Reference:
(http://en.wikipedia.org/wiki/Hitler_and_Mannerheim_recording)

251.

The first interracial kiss on American network television is often attributed to a 1968 episode of Star Trek, "Plato's Stepchildren". Though, Shatner claims that he and Nichols' lips never fully touched, while Nichols has alternately asserted that the kiss was, in fact, real.

Reference:
(https://en.wikipedia.org/wiki/First_interracial_kiss_on_television)

252.

After buying out the McDonalds brothers, Ray Kroc was angry that the deal did not include the original McDonalds, so he forced the McDonald brothers to change the name of the establishment to Big M and opened a McDonalds a block away to put them out of business.

Reference: (https://www.entrepreneur.com/article/197544)

253.

The German invasion of Denmark during World War II lasted only 6 hours.

Reference:
(https://en.wikipedia.org/wiki/German_invasion_of_Denmark_(1940
))

254.

In 1998, Fox aired a television movie called Nick Fury: Agent of S.H.I.E.L.D, with David Hasselhoff starring as Nick Fury.

Reference:
(https://en.wikipedia.org/wiki/Nick_Fury:_Agent_of_S.H.I.E.L.D._(film))

255.

The alphabet is called the alphabet because "alpha" and "beta" are the first two letters of the Greek alphabet.

Reference: (http://en.wikipedia.org/wiki/Alphabet)

256.

In 2008, PayPal cofounder Peter Thiel invested in an institute whose goal was to create man-made islands in unregulated international waters.

Reference: (http://www.wired.com/2015/05/silicon-valley-letting-go-techie-island-fantasies/)

257.

In 1976, footballer Chris Nicholl scored all 4 goals in a game that ended in a draw.

Reference:
(https://en.wikipedia.org/wiki/Chris_Nicholl#Playing_career)

258.

A man paralyzed from his elbows down was able to move his hand again, due to a chip implanted in his brain. The chip transmits brain signals to a sleeve with 130 electrodes that stimulate and contract hand muscles.

Reference: (http://www.bbc.com/news/health-36015248)

259.

The Rainbow Herbicides are a category of tactical chemicals used in the Vietnam War. The different chemicals were named after various colors, with the most known being Agent Orange.

Reference: (https://en.wikipedia.org/wiki/Rainbow_Herbicides)

260.

Medieval peasants got more vacation time than modern workers.

Reference: (http://nypost.com/2013/09/04/medieval-peasants-got-a-lot-more-vacation-time-than-you-economist/)

261.

At the close of the Second Opium War between the U.K. and China, U.K. troops looted and destroyed the Summer Palace in Peking, which is modern Beijing. Among the many treasures were 5 Pekingese dogs who were taken back to England where one of the dogs was given to Queen Victory and named "Looty".

Reference: (https://mimimatthews.com/2015/05/22/looty-the-pekingese-and-the-destruction-of-the-summer-palace/)

262.

When using inhalants, the heart becomes so sensitized to adrenaline, that you can literally be scared to death.

Reference:
(https://en.wikipedia.org/wiki/Inhalant#Sudden_sniffing_death_syndrome)

263.

Iceland, strategically located in the northern Atlantic, once threatened to leave NATO because of the Cod Wars, which was a conflict between the U.K. and Iceland over fishing rights.

Reference: (https://en.wikipedia.org/wiki/Cod_Wars)

264.

There exists a portion of New York State fully landlocked within the state of New Jersey.

Reference:
(https://en.wikipedia.org/wiki/New_Jersey_v._New_York)

265.

Our brains react to real life interaction very similarly to when we are reading about fictional interactions.

Reference: (http://wordservewatercooler.com/2012/06/22/does-reading-fiction-affect-your-brain/)

266.

In 1980, an oil drilling rig in Louisiana tapped into a salt mine and suddenly drained a 1,300 acre lake.

Reference: (https://www.damninteresting.com/lake-peigneur-the-swirling-vortex-of-doom/)

267.

Squirrels have a pointy bone in their penises.

Reference: (https://youtu.be/4iko2eExc08?t=2m22s)

268.

The Land of Towers in the Caucasus was 14 villages where every house was a fortress.

Reference: (http://www.atlasofwonders.com/2016/01/caucasus-towers-georgia-ingushetia.html)

269.

The Crown Jewels of Russia spent over 30 years in Ireland as collateral for a loan granted by the Irish Republicans to the New Russian Republic.

Reference:
(https://en.wikipedia.org/wiki/Imperial_Crown_of_Russia)

270.

The most complex molecule known to man; fullerene "carbon onions," may be commonplace throughout our universe and could act as transport vessels for key molecules and atoms which are precursors to life.

Reference:
(http://www.iac.es/divulgacion.php?op1=16&id=782&lang=en)

271.

Oliver Stone initially saw the Natural Born Killers script as an action film; "something Arnold Schwarzenegger would be proud of."

Reference:
(https://en.wikipedia.org/wiki/Natural_Born_Killers#Production)

272.

Former U.S. President Jimmy Carter helped clean up radioactive contamination from a nuclear meltdown in Canada.

Reference:
(https://en.wikipedia.org/wiki/Chalk_River_Laboratories)

273.

The British RAF in World War II started a propaganda campaign that eating carrots improved your eyesight. They did this so the Nazis wouldn't suspect the RAF's use of radar.

Reference: (http://www.snopes.com/food/ingredient/carrots.asp)

274.

Professional football player Rob Konrad was fishing off the coast of Florida when his boat capsized. Over a 16 hour period, he experienced hypothermia, multiple jellyfish stings, and at one point, was circled by a shark. He survived by swimming 9 miles back to shore.

Reference: (https://en.wikipedia.org/wiki/Rob_Konrad)

275.

In 2001, British author Giles Foden, best known for his novel "Last King of Scotland", compared Eminem to Robert Browning, one of the foremost Victorian poets. Foden remarked that a "brief examination of "Stan" reveals it to have all the depth and texture of the greatest examples of English verse."

Reference: (http://usatoday30.usatoday.com/life/music/news/2011-02-04-eminembard04_ST_N.htm)

276.

In 1982, as a protest against actions by the United States federal government, Key West in Florida seceded from and then declared war on the United States, surrendered one minute later and then applied for one billion dollars in foreign aid.

Reference: (http://holeinthedonut.com/2009/04/24/key-west-florida-conch-republic/)

277.

The idea of directed panspermia, which suggests that Earth was seeded by aliens, was suggested by Nobel Prize winner Francis Crick, a molecular biologist, who was also the co-discoverer of the structure of DNA in 1953.

Reference: (http://www.huffingtonpost.com/2015/02/03/aliens-send-space-seed-to-earth_n_6608582.html)

278.

Sex toys were illegal in apartheid South Africa.

Reference:
(https://en.wikisource.org/wiki/Immorality_Amendment_Act,_1969)

279.

There's a chemical, denatonium benzoate, which is used to control cannibalism among pigs, due to its extraordinarily bitter flavor.

Reference: (http://www.cpsc.gov//PageFiles/96066/aversive.pdf)

280.

There is a stuffed animal hospital that cleans and repairs beloved stuffed animals and dolls. The toys are called patients, shipped in an ambulance box, and returned wearing a hospital bracelet with their name.

Reference:
(http://www.stuffedanimals.com/stuffed_animal_hospital_a/164.htm
)

281.

Rapper J.Cole received his post-secondary degree diploma 8 years after graduation because he didn't pay off his fines for an overdue library book.

Reference: (http://hypetrak.com/2015/04/j-cole-finally-receives-his-college-diploma-8-years-since-graduation/)

282.

Associated Press entered a formal cooperation with Hitler's Nazi Germany, supplying American newspapers with material selected and produced by the Nazi party propaganda ministry.

Reference: (https://en.wikipedia.org/wiki/Associated_Press)

283.

Clouds typically weigh about a million pounds.

Reference: (http://chemistry.about.com/od/geochemistry/fl/How-Much-Does-a-Cloud-Weigh.htm)

284.

A single Finnish man hid in the Finland forests during World War II and killed over 500 Soviets in less than 100 days. He was nicknamed

"White Death" by the Soviets and they focused missions entirely on him.

Reference:
(https://en.wikipedia.org/wiki/Simo_H%C3%A4yh%C3%A4)

285.

Ruth Lawrence, a child prodigy, passed the Oxford University math exam at age 10, coming first out of all 530 candidates, she then completed the degree a year early, by age 13.

Reference: (http://en.wikipedia.org/wiki/Ruth_Lawrence)

286.

Italic and Oblique type are not the same thing. Oblique type is simply the normal font slanted to the right, while Italic also has slightly different character stylings.

Reference: (http://creativepro.com/typetalk-italic-vs-oblique/)

287.

The movie, "The Hangover," is named "Very Bad Trip" in France.

Reference: (https://fr.wikipedia.org/wiki/Very_Bad_Trip)

288.

It is legal to open carry a sword in California, but only if it's sheathed.

Reference: (http://blogs.findlaw.com/blotter/2014/02/is-it-legal-to-carry-a-sword-in-public.html)

289.

Since 1989, Gallup polling has found that in most years in which there was a decline in the U.S. crime rate, a majority of Americans said that violent crime was getting worse.

Reference:
(https://en.wikipedia.org/wiki/United_States_incarceration_rate)

290.

There was a secret society for Catholics called "The Order of the Pug." Novices were initiated by wearing a dog collar and they had to scratch at the door to get in.

Reference: (https://en.wikipedia.org/wiki/Order_of_the_Pug)

291.

Mia Khalifa, a famous pornstar, worked at a Whataburger, where she was approached by a customer to enter the porn industry.

Reference: (https://en.wikipedia.org/wiki/Mia_Khalifa)

292.

Farmers who called their cows by name reported 258 liter higher milk yield than those who did not.

Reference:
(http://www.ncl.ac.uk/press/news/legacy/2012/01/namesgivecowsalo
ttabottle.html)

293.

Life on Earth contains elevated levels of radioactive carbon, C14, from above-ground nuclear tests of the 1950s and 1960s. C14 levels have steadily decreased, allowing scientists to measure the age of cells in humans, and prove that parts of the brain regenerate.

Reference: (http://www.pbs.org/wgbh/nova/next/body/bomb-pulse/)

294.

Mfecane Mfecane or Lifaqane, was a period of widespread chaos and warfare among indigenous ethnic communities in Southern Africa during the period between 1815 and 1840.

Reference: (https://en.wikipedia.org/wiki/Mfecane)

295.

The King of Thailand is the world's longest reigning monarch, with having ruled for 69 years. He is also the richest, with a net worth of $30 billion dollars.

Reference: (http://www.bbc.co.uk/news/world-asia-30341182)

296.

The longest-lasting musical performances yet undertaken began on September 5th, 2001, with a pause lasting until February 5th, 2003. The last note change occurred on October 5th, 2013. The next change will not occur until 2020. The performance is scheduled to end on September 5th, 2640.

Reference: (https://en.wikipedia.org/wiki/As_Slow_as_Possible)

297.

Bollywood actor Sharukh Khan, also known as King Khan, is the second richest actor in the world with a net worth of $600 million, surpassing actors such as Tom Cruise and Johnny Depp. Jerry Seinfeld is the richest actor in the world.

Reference:
(https://www.theguardian.com/film/2014/may/21/bollywood-shah-rukh-khan-actor)

298.

If the blood vessels, arteries, veins and capillaries, of an adult were lined up end to end, which would measure close to 100,000 miles, they would circle the equator, close to 25,000 miles, four times.

Reference: (http://www.madsci.org/posts/archives/1999-01/916069852.An.r.html)

299.

The phrase "Smart Alec" arose from the exploits of one Alec Hoag, who was a celebrated pimp, thief, and confidence man operating out of New York City in the 1840s.

Reference: (http://mentalfloss.com/article/32046/where-did-phrase-smart-alec-come)

300.

If people in the 10% for alcohol consumption were to reduce their total consumption to that of the next lowest 10% group; alcohol sales would drop by 60% in the U.S.

Reference:
(http://www.washingtonpost.com/blogs/wonkblog/wp/2014/09/25/think-you-drink-a-lot-this-chart-will-tell-you/)

301.

Australia uses the motion of the ocean to generate zero-emission electricity and desalinate water simultaneously.

Reference: (http://magazine.good.is/articles/australia-ceto-water-power-wave-generator)

302.

Bamboo is actually the largest type of grass in the world and can sometimes grow as fast as 1 millimeter every 90 seconds.

Reference: (https://en.wikipedia.org/wiki/Bamboo)

303.

Standing at 7"6', 15-year-old teen basketball giant Robert Bobroczky is already taller than any current NBA player.

Reference: (http://www.cbc.ca/sports/basketball/nba/robert-bobroczky-romanian-basketball-1.3371573)

304.

Trees can die from something unpleasant getting sucked up in their roots which gets caught in the phloem and xylem. It's very similar to getting a piece of food caught in your throat.

Reference: (http://zidbits.com/2012/08/do-trees-die-from-old-age/)

305.

At the age of 5 years and 11 months, Ayan Qureshi took and passed Microsoft's IT Technician Exam, making him the youngest certified computer specialist in the world.

Reference: (http://thehigherlearning.com/2014/11/17/a-5-year-old-boy-just-passed-microsofts-it-technician-exam/)

306.

Excessive lactose in the small intestine attracts water molecules through osmosis, causing diarrhea for people with lactose intolerance.

Reference: (http://www.livestrong.com/article/468012-why-does-lactose-intolerance-cause-diarrhea/)

307.

During Gettysburg, despite it being the largest battle ever fought in the western hemisphere with more than 165,000 soldiers engaged and more than 46,000 casualties on both sides, only 1 civilian was killed, a 20 year old seamstress named Ginnie Wade.

Reference: (https://en.wikipedia.org/wiki/Ginnie_Wade)

308.

Cavalry were used to great effect in the Portuguese Colonial War, from 1966 to 1975.

Reference: (https://en.wikipedia.org/wiki/Dragoons_of_Angola)

309.

A Japanese man married a Nintendo DS character in 2009.

Reference:(http://www.dailytech.com/Japanese+Man+Marries+Video+Game+Character/article16953.htm)

310.

In 1994, the Rolling Stones were the first major group to stream a concert live on the Internet. However, since the technology was so new, only 200 computers were able to watch it.

Reference: (http://www.nytimes.com/1994/11/22/arts/rolling-stones-live-on-internet-both-a-big-deal-and-a-little-deal.html)

311.

The word "media" is the plural form of "medium".

Reference: (http://www.dictionary.com/browse/media)

312.

The Basque language is the only isolate language of Western Europe. It is not related to Spanish, French, or any other known language.

Reference: (https://en.wikipedia.org/wiki/Basque_language)

313.

In the 1600's, tulips cost ten times what an average working-class man earned in a year.

Reference: (http://www.teleflora.com/blog/10-weird-facts-about-tulips/)

314.

The song, "New York, New York," usually sung by Frank Sinatra, was written because of Robert De Niro. He was in a movie with the song as the title song and insisted that it was re-written because he didn't like it. The writers were angry when he insisted but rewrote it to be the classic that we know today.

Reference: (http://www.npr.org/2015/11/25/457289950/broadway-composer-john-kander-reflects-on-a-career-of-hidden-treasures)

315.

Suggs, singer in the band "Madness", learned that his father was dead after reading his own Wikipedia page.

Reference: (https://en.wikipedia.org/wiki/Suggs_(singer))

316.

The Terror Bird id a 10 foot tall bird that killed its prey by shattering its bones and stunning it with its beak.

Reference: (https://en.wikipedia.org/wiki/Phorusrhacidae)

317.

Prora is a hotel at the German island of Rügen in the Baltic Sea. It stretches over a staggering three miles and has 10,000 bedrooms all facing the sea. It was constructed on the orders of Hitler.

Reference: (https://en.wikipedia.org/wiki/Prora)

318.

The fastest-ever recorded mile run by a human was 3:28.36 by Mike Boit in 1983, on the downhill "Queen Street Golden Mile" course in New Zealand.

Reference: (http://spikes.iaaf.org/post/golden-queen-street-mile)

319.

Architect Eero Saarinen, who designed the Gateway Arch, the Washington Dulles International Airport, and the TWA Flight center as examples, inspired the design of Star Trek, General Motors, IBM, John Deere and CBS.

Reference: (http://io9.gizmodo.com/5402867/the-space-age-designs-that-inspired-star-trek--and-corporate-america/)

320.

The Beatles played a demo copy of "Sgt. Pepper's Lonely Hearts Club Band" before its release at full volume from an open apartment window at 6AM. Instead of complaining, the residents opened their windows and listened, aware that they were hearing unreleased Beatles music.

Reference:(http://en.wikipedia.org/wiki/Sgt._Pepper%27s_Lonely_Hearts_Club_Band#Cover_artwork)

321.

The liqueur Curaçao is made from orange trees brought to the Caribbean from Spain in 1527. The trees failed to thrive and were abandoned. The fruit evolved from sweet orange into bitter green. Experimentation with dried peels of the fruit later led to the creation of the liqueur Curaçao.

Reference: (https://en.wikipedia.org/wiki/Laraha)

322.

Samy, from the infamous Amy's Baking Company that appeared on Kitchen Nightmares, threatened to kill a drunk customer with a knife outside their restaurant.

Reference:
(http://www.azcentral.com/story/news/local/scottsdale/2014/09/28/amys-baking-company-knife-incident-abrk/16400137/)

323.

A band named the "Imperial Stars" blocked traffic on the 101 Freeway in Hollywood with their truck, then began singing and playing instruments on top in an impromptu performance entitled "Traffic Jam 101". California Highway Patrol arrived shortly after and arrested 3 band members.

Reference: (http://latimesblogs.latimes.com/lanow/2010/10/band-members-arrested-after-blocking-101-freeway-for-performance.html)

324.

The words "For Our Princess" are engraved inside every Microsoft Zune HD as a tribute to a team member who passed away during its development.

Reference: (https://www.ifixit.com/Teardown/Microsoft-Zune-HD/1170/1#s6210)

325.

The chills experienced when listening to music is a result of the brain releasing dopamine in anticipation of the peak moment during a song.

Reference: (http://news.discovery.com/human/psychology/music-dopamine-happiness-brain-110110.htm)

326.

HyperCard was created after a programmer had a LSD trip.

Reference: (https://en.wikipedia.org/wiki/HyperCard#History)

327.

Dracunculiasis, also known as Guinea-worm disease, is caused by the Guinea worm, which can grow up to 1 meter long inside a human host.

Reference: (https://en.wikipedia.org/wiki/Dracunculiasis)

328.

A man attempted to jump off of the 86th floor of the Empire State Building, only to hit the catwalk on the floor below it.

Reference: (http://abcnews.go.com/blogs/headlines/2013/04/man-survives-fall-from-empire-state-building-after-landing-on-catwalk/)

329.

In 1255, King Henry III of England received an elephant from King Louis IX of France. It died in 1257 from drinking too much red wine.

Reference:
(https://en.wikipedia.org/wiki/History_of_elephants_in_Europe)

330.

52% of American's can't afford the house that they are currently living in right now.

Reference:(http://www.marketwatch.com/story/over-50-of-americans-struggle-with-home-affordability-2014-06-03)

331.

Discovery Channel has its own telescope called the Discovery Channel Telescope (DCT).

Reference:
(https://en.wikipedia.org/wiki/Discovery_Channel_Telescope)

332.

J. Cole graduated college in 2007, but didn't receive his diploma until 8 years later because he owed money for a library book that he never paid for.

Reference: (https://en.wikipedia.org/wiki/J._Cole)

333.

The last attempt at a Constitutional Amendment to be submitted to the states was approved in 1978, marking the longest period in which Congress has not approved a single amendment since the Civil War.

Reference:(https://en.wikipedia.org/wiki/List_of_proposed_amendments_to_the_United_States_Constitution)

334.

In 2011, scientists at UC Berkeley were able to reconstruct images seen by a patient by scanning their brain with an MRI scan and running the data through a program.

Reference:(https://www.youtube.com/watch?v=6FsH7RK1S2E&feature=youtu.be&ab_channel=UCBerkeley)

335.

The USS Arizona that was destroyed in the Pearl Harbor attack, still leaks fuel to this day.

Reference: (https://en.wikipedia.org/wiki/USS_Arizona_Memorial)

336.

Theodore Streleski killed his Ph.D. advisor at Stanford after failing to get his Ph.D. after 19 years.

Reference:
(http://www.people.com/people/archive/article/0,,20091783,00.html)

337.

Somebody bought the rusted War Games movie WOPR computer, in 2012 for an estimated bid of $20,000.00.

Reference: (http://www.icollector.com/War-Games-Original-WOPR-Computer_i13855776)

338.

In 1891, after two trains collided in Connecticut, a third collided with the two. Five minutes later, a fourth train collided with the three.

Reference:
(https://en.wikipedia.org/wiki/Great_East_Thompson_Train_Wreck)

339.

In the last 53 years, 10 actors have played the role of Ronald McDonald.

Reference:
(http://mcdonalds.wikia.com/wiki/Actors_who_have_played_Ronald_McDonald)

340.

Earth produces $72 trillion dollars' worth of goods each year.

Reference: (http://news.thomasnet.com/imt/2012/06/23/how-much-is-nature-worth-how-about-72-trillion-a-year)

341.

NASA has a document for other companies planning moon landings to help avoid disturbing the historic Apollo sites.

Reference: (https://www.nasa.gov/pdf/617743main_NASA-USG_LUNAR_HISTORIC_SITES_RevA-508.pdf)

342.

On his second day in office, Jimmy Carter issued unconditional pardons to hundreds of thousands of Vietnam War draft dodgers.

Reference: (http://www.politico.com/story/2008/01/carter-pardons-draft-dodgers-jan-21-1977-007974)

343.

Menthol cigarettes are so popular among black Americans that black groups opposed a proposed ban as a civil rights issue.

Reference:
(http://www.theatlantic.com/health/archive/2011/03/mint-that-kills-the-curious-life-of-menthol-cigarettes/73016/)

344.

The Stanley Cup was established in 1892 by the Governor General of Canada, Lord Stanley of Preston, and isn't actually owned by the NHL and can even possibly be awarded to teams outside of the NHL.

Reference: (https://thenib.com/meet-the-stanley-cup-704c3c5a39c8#.w5wl2ow3h)

345.

Cockroaches experience performance anxiety. A study found that cockroaches running through a hard maze will have more difficulties if other roaches are watching them.

Reference:
(http://en.wikipedia.org/wiki/Social_facilitation#Activation_theory)

346.

There is a civilian calendar for Mars called the Darian Calendar. Tosol, which is the Martian "today", is Gemini 8, 216.

Reference: (https://en.wikipedia.org/wiki/Darian_calendar)

347.

Atlanto-occipital dislocation, or internal decapitation, is an injury in which the spinal column separates from the base of the skull, which is immediately fatal 70% of the time.

Reference: (https://en.wikipedia.org/wiki/Atlanto-occipital_dislocation)

348.

The dice game "Bunco", popular today with families, is historically associated with gambling and swindles. The term "Bunco Squad" for police comes from raids on illegal gambling parlors using the game.

Reference: (https://en.wikipedia.org/wiki/Bunco)

349.

The stereotypical nonchalance of Italian men is called "Sprezzatura."

Reference: (https://en.wikipedia.org/wiki/Sprezzatura?1)

350.

A Russian 4 year old left his abusive parents to live with a pack of wild dogs. Before his capture by police, he became the pack leader and escaped authorities three times. He later studied in Military School and served in the Russian Army.

Reference: (http://en.wikipedia.org/wiki/Ivan_Mishukov)

351.

There's a tree that grows 40 different types of fruit.

Reference: (http://www.cnn.com/2015/08/03/living/tree-40-fruit-sam-van-aken-feat/)

352.

Scientists diagnosed a 2250-year old Egyptian mummy with metastatic prostate cancer.

Reference: (http://www.sciencemag.org/news/2011/10/mummy-has-oldest-case-prostate-cancer-ancient-egypt)

353.

There is a super rare blood type called RH Null that only around 10 to 40 people in the world have.

Reference: (http://www.newser.com/story/197796/what-its-like-to-have-the-golden-blood-type.html)

354.

In the 18th century, it was common to literally blow smoke up someone's rectum for resuscitation and to treat a variety of medical conditions.

Reference: (http://www.historyextra.com/qa/smoke-it-out)

355.

A professor of medical psychology in New York started hearing a voice in her head in 1965. Her colleague encouraged her to write down what it said. The voice produced 3 volumes of "spiritual psychology," some of which is written in iambic pentameter.

Reference: (http://en.wikipedia.org/wiki/A_Course_in_Miracles)

356.

The Olm, a blind cave salamander, can go over a decade without eating by cooling down its metabolism when it senses there is no food.

Reference: (http://io9.gizmodo.com/this-animal-can-go-over-a-decade-without-food-1723304968)

357.

The number in the triangle on plastic containers dictates whether the item can be reused or recycled.

Reference: (http://learn.eartheasy.com/2012/05/plastics-by-the-numbers/)

358.

Cookies originated from Persia.

Reference: (https://en.wikipedia.org/wiki/Cookie#History)

359.

Darth Vader's costume was largely inspired by the Fighting Devil Dogs villain "The Lightning" who also had white Stormtroopers and flew in a triangular ship.

Reference:
(https://en.wikipedia.org/wiki/Star_Wars_sources_and_analogues)

360.

In 1969, Marvel created the Squadron Sinister, a team of supervillains whose members' abilities mirrored Superman, Batman, Green Lantern, the Flash, and Wonder Woman, as punching bags for The Avengers.

Reference: (http://thepopcultist.com/2013/05/26/the-squadron-sinister-marvels-cheap-justice-league-knock-offs/)

361.

The Weather Company is owned by IBM, it licenses out The Weather Channel name and branding to NBCUniversal.

Reference: (https://en.wikipedia.org/wiki/The_Weather_Company)

362.

Brie Larson released a pop album "Finally Out of P.E." in 2005, which flopped by selling only 3,500 copies. Larson even toured with Jesse McCartney for Teen People's Rock in Shop Tour.

Reference: (https://en.wikipedia.org/wiki/Finally_Out_of_P.E.)

363.

Jeff Bridges said of working on Iron Man, "They had no script, man. We would show up for big scenes every day and we wouldn't know what we were going to say. We would go into our trailer and call up writers on the phone, 'You got any ideas?'"

Reference: (http://io9.gizmodo.com/5417310/jeff-bridges-admits-iron-man-movie-had-no-script)

364.

Larry David inadvertently saved a man from his death row sentence by accidentally filming him during a scene at Dodger Stadium that provided the defendant a solid alibi.

Reference: (http://www.cnn.com/2004/LAW/06/07/larry.david/)

365.

The Nova Scotia Government sends Boston a 40 to 50 foot Christmas tree every single year, as a symbol of remembrance for the aid they gave after the Halifax explosion.

Reference: (http://www.cbc.ca/strombo/news/every-year-nova-scotia-sends-boston-a-tree-to-say-thanks)

366.

The original "Airwolf" helicopter, from the 1980s television series, was sold to a German company, became an air-ambulance and crashed, killing its 3 occupants.

Reference: (https://en.wikipedia.org/wiki/Airwolf_(helicopter))

367.

Nitrous, a chemical used to boost the power output of an engine, is also called laughing gas.

Reference: (https://en.wikipedia.org/wiki/Nitrous_oxide)

368.

Exploding Head Syndrome is a condition in which a person hears loud imagined noises when falling asleep or waking up.

Reference:
(https://en.wikipedia.org/wiki/Exploding_head_syndrome)

369.

92 Senegalese troops died in the Gulf War Coalition, which is second only to United States casualties.

Reference: (https://en.wikipedia.org/wiki/Gulf_War)

370.

An 18th century astronomer went to India to see a Transit of Venus. Delayed, he missed it, but decided to stay for the next one, which occurred in 8 years. The second try was clouded out so 3 years later, he returned home. When he came back to France, he found that he had been declared dead, his wife had remarried and his estate was gone.

Reference: (http://messier.seds.org/xtra/Bios/legentil.html)

371.

There is a marvel super villain called The Russian.

Reference: (https://en.wikipedia.org/wiki/Russian_(comics))

372.

Lobsters continuously grow, become more fertile, and show no signs of biological aging as they grow older.

Reference: (http://www.csmonitor.com/Science/2011/0616/How-large-can-lobsters-grow-Big!-But-no-one-knows-how-big)

373.

Steam-powered cars are exempt from road tax.

Reference: (https://www.gov.uk/vehicle-exempt-from-vehicle-tax)

374.

In the Queen song, "One Vision", the last two words of the lyrics officially claim to be "one vision." However, in the actual song, the last two words Freddie Mercury says is "Fried Chicken."

Reference:
(https://en.wikipedia.org/wiki/One_Vision#.22Fried_chicken.22)

375.

John Lennon once called an 'emergency board meeting' of the Beatles in order to inform his band mates that he'd realized, while tripping on acid, that he was the second coming of Jesus.

Reference:(http://www.csicop.org/specialarticles/show/when_the_beatles_were_bigger_than_jesus_christ/)

376.

At the age of 12, Jay Z shot his drug addicted brother over a ring that was stolen.

Reference: (http://www.nydailynews.com/entertainment/gossip/jay-z-speaks-shooting-drug-addict-brother-age-12-new-memoir-decoded-article-1.452765)

377.

Until 1980, there were only two bridges across the Yangtze River in China. Today there are 136.

Reference:
(https://en.wikipedia.org/wiki/Bridges_and_tunnels_across_the_Yangtze_River)

378.

In 1992, there was a CIS football team entry to the EURO 1992.

Reference:
(https://en.wikipedia.org/wiki/CIS_national_football_team)

379.

Most mirrors are slightly green.

Reference: (http://www.livescience.com/34427-what-color-is-a-mirror.html)

380.

The New Madrid fault created a massive earthquake a couple centuries ago, causing the Mississippi to flow backwards in 1811 - 1812. This backwards flow created Reelfoot Lake in North Tennessee.

Reference:
(http://en.wikipedia.org/wiki/1811%E2%80%9312_New_Madrid_earthquakes)

381.

Uncompleted tasks are easier to remember than finished ones, thus making cliffhangers in movies stick longer in a person's mind.

Reference: (https://en.wikipedia.org/wiki/Zeigarnik_effect)

382.

26 year old Kyle MacDonald was able to trade a single red paperclip all the way up to a house, using the "Bigger and Better" game strategy.

Reference:
(http://abcnews.go.com/Technology/story?id=2192233&page=1)

383.

The Foxhound forced the Blackbird into retirement by the end of the 1980s.

Reference:(http://in.rbth.com/articles/2012/09/03/foxhound_vs_blac kbird_how_the_migs_reclaimed_the_skies_17363)

384.

After "shake it like a Polaroid" became part of a hit song, Polaroid warned customers that this could actually destroy their photographs.

Reference:
(http://www.cnn.com/2004/TECH/ptech/02/17/polaroid.warns.reut/i ndex.html)

385.

After D.B. Cooper's hijacking, the flight crew claimed that he was very calm and kind. After he hijacked the plane with a bomb threat, he ordered a drink, paid the tab, and even tipped the flight attendant. Cooper also offered to request meals for crew members as part of his ransom request.

Reference: (https://en.wikipedia.org/wiki/D._B._Cooper#Hijacking)

386.

In 1962, when Mercury astronaut John Glenn conducted eating experiments in orbit, Tang was selected for the menu; it was also used during some Gemini flights. In 2013, Buzz Aldrin said: "Tang sucks".

Reference: (http://www.npr.org/sections/thetwo-way/2013/06/13/191271824/now-he-tells-us-tang-sucks-says-apollo-11s-buzz-aldrin)

387.

Ottomans Subs where the first in the world to fire a live torpedo under water.

Reference:
(https://en.wikipedia.org/wiki/Ottoman_submarine_Abd%C3%BCl_Hamid)

388.

Peter Jackson began filming The Hobbit trilogy without proper preparation, in many cases shooting scenes without storyboards and completed scripts in a process he described as, "making it up as I went along".

Reference: (https://youtu.be/20vA9U7J2qQ)

389.

The United States Navy requested that the Golden Gate Bridge initially be painted black with yellow stripes. The color "International Orange" was later selected because it enhanced visibility in fog.

Reference:
(https://en.wikipedia.org/wiki/Golden_Gate_Bridge#Design)

390.

Apollo 15 astronaut, Al Worden, wrote a book of poems about his trip to the Moon.

Reference: (https://archive.org/details/HelloEarth)

391.

Former Rolling Stones producer Jimmy Miller replaced drummer Charlie Watts on "You Can't Always Get What You Want." The change was made after Watts was unable to figure out the beat for the song's unusual groove and rhythm.

Reference:(https://en.wikipedia.org/wiki/You_Can%27t_Always_Get_What_You_Want#Description)

392.

The letters and numbers in a hex code represent the red, green, and blue values. 00 representing no color intensity and FF representing 255 the highest intensity.

Reference: (http://htmlcolorcodes.com/)

393.

On August 16th, 1996, at Brookfield Zoo, a 3 year-old boy fell into a gorilla enclosure and lost consciousness. Binti Jua, a female gorilla, guarded the young boy from the other gorillas, cradled him in her arms and carried him 60 feet to an entrance where zookeepers could retrieve him.

Reference: (http://upliftingdaily.com/10-heroic-animals-who-saved-human-lives/)

394.

The Director of the Brain Tumor Surgery Program, the Pituitary Surgery Program, and the Brain Tumor Stem Cell Laboratory at Johns Hopkins Hospital was an undocumented immigrant from Mexico who first worked as a migrant farmer in Fresno, California.

Reference: (https://en.wikipedia.org/wiki/Alfredo_Quinones-Hinojosa)

395.

Robert Louis Stevenson, author of Treasure Island, formally donated his birthday by deed of gift to a friend's daughter who was born on Christmas Day and had no birthday celebration separate from the family's Christmas celebrations.

Reference:
(http://en.wikipedia.org/wiki/Robert_Louis_Stevenson#Last_years)

396.

Bamboo sharks can survive on land for 12 hours, and have known to have virgin births.

Reference:
(https://en.wikipedia.org/wiki/Brownbanded_bamboo_shark)

397.

Paul Erdős, one of the most prolific mathematicians in history, remained unconvinced of the solution to the Monty Hall problem until he was shown a computer simulation confirming the result.

Reference: (https://en.wikipedia.org/wiki/Monty_Hall_problem)

398.

The South Park team begins episode production only a week before the air date, including script writing. Sometimes they even send the episode over just a few hours before it airs.

Reference: (http://wikipedia.org/wiki/South_Park#production)

399.

Qatar FIFA World Cup migrant death figures are actually misleading because they include all deaths of migrants, whether that's relating to the World Cup or not.

Reference: (http://www.bbc.co.uk/news/magazine-33019838)

400.

Despite being on hard times, one of the US most decorated war veterans repeatedly turned down offers to appear in Alcohol and Tobacco commercials because he knew it would be a bad role model for young people. The soldier, Audie Murphy, had earned every single US Army Award for combat in World War II.

Reference: (https://en.wikipedia.org/wiki/Audie_Murphy)

401.

Garrett P. Serviss wrote a sequel to War of the Worlds and is arguably the first American to write science fiction professionally.

Reference:
(https://en.wikipedia.org/wiki/Edison%27s_Conquest_of_Mars)

402.

When the U.S. Navy banned alcohol on ships in July, 1914, they held one last massive party and invited ships from several nations to help drink the last of the booze. Many of the participants in the party would become enemies weeks later when World War I broke out.

Reference: (https://news.usni.org/2014/07/01/hundred-years-dry-u-s-navys-end-alcohol-sea)

403.

The Earth's atmosphere also has tides.

Reference: (https://en.wikipedia.org/wiki/Atmospheric_tide)

404.

Boarding an airplane in random order is approximately 7 minutes faster than boarding the plane back-to-front.

Reference: (http://culturegeographic.com/2016/01/16/better-way-board-airplane/)

405.

Cold is contagious. In a new study, when subjects looked at someone dipping their hands into ice water, their own hands actually grew colder.

Reference:(http://www.realclearscience.com/journal_club/2015/01/03/cold_is_contagious_109007.html)

406.

With only about 56 inhabitants, originating from four main families, Pitcairn is the least populous national jurisdiction in the world. The United Nations Committee on Decolonization includes the Pitcairn Islands on the United Nations list of Non-Self-Governing Territories.

Reference: (https://en.wikipedia.org/wiki/Pitcairn_Islands)

407.

The infamous "Chili Finger Lady", Anna Ayala, has a long history of suing people and jail time.

Reference: (https://en.wikipedia.org/wiki/Anna_Ayala)

408.

John Adams, before becoming the second U.S. President, was the lawyer who defended the British soldiers responsible for the Boston

Massacre. Six of the soldiers were acquitted, while the other two were convicted of manslaughter and given reduced sentences.

Reference: (https://en.wikipedia.org/wiki/Boston_Massacre#Trials)

409.

After the WWE held a televised tribute to Chris Benoit, and the circumstances surrounding his murder and suicide were revealed, the WWE has taken steps to remove most of his history with the company, including editing him out of archived footage and video games.

Reference: (https://en.wikipedia.org/wiki/Chris_Benoit_double-murder_and_suicide#World_Wrestling_Entertainment)

410.

All the War Boys in Mad Max are inbred and have at least one form of cancer.

Reference:
(http://madmax.wikia.com/wiki/War_Boys#Health_issues)

411.

Hugh Jackman was a last second choice to play Wolverine in the X-Men movie. He was cast three weeks into filming after his successful audition.

Reference: (https://en.wikipedia.org/wiki/X-Men_%28film%29)

412.

Kanye West hasn't had a number 1 single on the Billboard Hot 100 in 9 years.

Reference: (https://en.wikipedia.org/wiki/Kanye_West_discography)

413.

Whirlpool is the only major appliance company to have gotten a perfect score on the Human Rights Campaign's Corporate Equality Index, which benchmarks policies related to LGBT equality, for over 10 years.

Reference: (http://www.prnewswire.com/news-releases/whirlpool-corporation-receives-perfect-score-on-human-rights-campaigns-corporate-equality-index-for-13th-consecutive-year-300180935.html)

414.

The show "Vikings" is loosely based off the legends of Bjorn Ironside and his father, Ragnar Lodbrok.

Reference: (https://en.wikipedia.org/wiki/Bj%C3%B6rn_Ironside)

415.

The Russians celebrated for so long after the end of World War II that the entire city of Moscow ran out of Vodka.

Reference: (http://mentalfloss.com/article/30351/time-russia-ran-out-vodka)

416.

Canadian generals' and admirals' ranks are denoted in Maple Leaves, not stars.

Reference:
(https://en.wikipedia.org/wiki/Canadian_Armed_Forces_ranks_and_insignia)

417.

Roger Hill, the actor who played Cyrus in The Warriors, took the part after a real life gang member mysteriously disappeared before filming.

Reference:
(https://en.wikipedia.org/wiki/Roger_Hill_%28actor%29)

418.

The parasite Toxoplasmosis gondii causes rats to become sexually attracted to cat urine.

Reference:
(http://www.ncbi.nlm.nih.gov/pmc/articles/PMC3157360/)

419.

When the GameBoy Camera was originally released, it was entered into the 1999 Guinness Book of Records for being the world's smallest digital camera.

Reference: (https://en.wikipedia.org/wiki/Game_Boy_Camera)

420.

Da Hong Pao is the most expensive tea in the world; at a cost of $1,025,000 per kilogram.

Reference: (http://en.wikipedia.org/wiki/Da_Hong_Pao)

421.

Antarctica was once covered in rich green forests and inhabited by dinosaurs, during one of Earth's warmest cycles.

Reference: (http://www.bbc.com/news/science-environment-12378934)

422.

There is an Arabic comic book featuring superheroes imbued with the powers of the 99 Names of God from the Qur'an.

Reference: (https://en.wikipedia.org/wiki/The_99)

423.

Maria Reynolds, who had an affair with Alexander Hamilton, sued her husband for divorce and her attorney was Aaron Burr.

Reference: (http://www.smithsonianmag.com/history/alexander-hamiltons-adultery-and-apology-18021947/?no-ist)

424.

A branch of socialism called "Libertarian Socialism" is close to the views of most Americans who call themselves socialists today. It advocates for worker rights, but opposes state ownership of the economy as a means to achieve that.

Reference: (https://en.wikipedia.org/wiki/Libertarian_socialism)

425.

Leonard Nimoy fought to get pay equity for Nichelle Nichols on Star Trek in the 1960s.

Reference: (http://trekmovie.com/2014/07/31/koenig-leonard-nimoy-fought-to-get-nichelle-nichols-pay-equity-for-star-trek-nimoy-confirms/)

426.

McDonald's adds beef flavor to their fries and hashbrowns and until 1990, they were fried in tallow.

Reference: (https://en.wikipedia.org/wiki/Tallow)

427.

Westinghouse operates half of the world's nuclear reactors; they purchased CBS in 1995, then sold the nuclear division to the British Government in 1999 which sold it in 2005 to Toshiba with a minority stake owned by Chicago Bridge and Iron Company and the country of Kazakhstan.

Reference:
(https://en.wikipedia.org/wiki/Westinghouse_Electric_Company)

428.

In the 1960s, the life expectancy in the Soviet Union surpassed that of the United States.

Reference: (https://en.wikipedia.org/wiki/Soviet_Union#Health)

429.

Brad Buxer collaborated with Michael Jackson and was a member of the band The Jetzons. In 1994, he worked on the soundtrack for Sonic the Hedgehog 3, which used instrumental versions of tracks recorded by Buxer and Jackson. A then-unreleased Jetzons song was also used.

Reference: (https://en.wikipedia.org/wiki/Brad_Buxer)

430.

Lego has no military related sets because the inventor's policy was to not want to make war seem like child's play.

Reference: (http://en.wikipedia.org/wiki/Lego#Sets)

431.

Major Allison Digby Tatham-Warter disabled a German armored car with his umbrella, incapacitating the driver by shoving the umbrella through the car's observational slit.

Reference: (https://en.wikipedia.org/wiki/Digby_Tatham-Warter)

432.

The largest flying animal that ever lived, the Quetzalcoatlus, had a wingspan of 10 meters.

Reference: (https://en.wikipedia.org/wiki/Quetzalcoatlus)

433.

The words "census" and "censorship" share the same root, since there was a Roman Senate officer in charge of both tasks.

Reference: (https://en.wikipedia.org/wiki/Roman_censor)

434.

20,000 Confederates immigrated to Brazil upon losing the American Civil War.

Reference: (https://en.wikipedia.org/wiki/Confederados)

435.

Sufiah Yusof is a genius child who enrolled at Oxford University at 12. She later became a prostitute, entertaining clients with her ability to recite equations during sexual acts.

Reference: (http://www.bbc.com/future/story/20150413-the-downsides-of-being-clever)

436.

An Arctic phenomenon called "superior mirage" allows cold air to bend light so that objects 250 miles away seem to be on the horizon.

Reference: (http://www.atoptics.co.uk/fz150.htm)

437.

A study found that a portable generator positioned 15 feet away from open windows was not far enough to prevent carbon monoxide entry into the house.

Reference: (http://www.nist.gov/el/highperformance_buildings/performance/generator_100609.cfm)

438.

In 1752, in England and Wales, people went to bed on the 2nd of September and woke up on the 14th of September. Skipping 11 days entirely because of the implementation of the Gregorian Calendar.

Reference: (http://mentalfloss.com/article/51370/why-our-calendars-skipped-11-days-1752)

439.

In 500 B.C.E., about one out of two people on Earth lived in the Archaemenid Empire. No empire in history would match this.

Reference: (https://en.wikipedia.org/wiki/Achaemenid_Empire)

440.

In 2005, OJ Simpson starred in a pay-per-view hidden camera show called, "Juiced." The show featured a prank wherein OJ tried to sell a used white Bronco, and the tag line was, "The Juice is on the loose ... again!"

Reference: (https://www.vice.com/read/i-was-oj-simpsons-accomplice-on-his-hidden-camera-prank-show-juiced)

441.

The Woodstock festival didn't actually take place in Woodstock.

Reference: (http://www.huffingtonpost.com/2013/11/25/woodstock-trivia_n_4334870.html)

442.

Kimbo Slice' son "Baby Slice" Kevin Ferguson Jr. also fights in MMA. His debut was in March.

Reference: (http://www.mmafighting.com/2016/3/25/11305912/video-kevin-ferguson-jr-son-of-kimbo-slice-scores-quick-ko-in-mma)

443.

Bomb and drug sniffing dogs will eventually develop psychological problems if they never find any, and must occasionally be taken on dummy missions to satisfy their "prey-drive."

Reference: (http://www.dogingtonpost.com/laser-pointers-could-be-bad-for-your-dog/)

444.

Stephen King considers his first novel to be "The Long Walk." The book is about 100 boys in a grueling walking contest where the winner is the last one to survive a never ending walk.

Reference: (https://en.wikipedia.org/wiki/The_Long_Walk)

445.

A German man broke into prison every single night to visit his girlfriend.

Reference: (http://www.spiegel.de/international/zeitgeist/punished-for-love-man-indicted-for-breaking-into-prison-a-678721.html)

446.

Female mice are massively underrepresented in drug testing trials, despite the fact that gender-specific reactions occur very frequently.

Reference: (https://www.researchgate.net/blog/post/where-are-the-female-mice-in-drug-testing)

447.

The part of Highway 401 that passes through Toronto is the busiest highway in the world.

Reference:
(http://international.fhwa.dot.gov/pubs/pl07027/llcp_07_02.cfm)

448.

Sir Ranulph Fiennes is the only man alive ever to have travelled around the Earth's circumpolar surface. His record-breaking expeditions include travel by riverboat, hovercraft, manhaul sledge, skidoo, Land Rover and ski.

Reference: (http://hobbyearth.com/gallery/6390)

449.

The character of Wong Fei-hung in the martial arts movies "Drunken Master" and "Iron Monkey" was a real person and over 100 movies and television series have been made about him.

Reference: (https://en.wikipedia.org/wiki/Wong_Fei-hung_filmography)

450.

Károly Takács, a right handed Hungarian shooter, severely injured his right (shooting) hand in a grenade explosion. He retrained himself with his left hand and went on to win 2 Olympic Gold's 10 years later.

Reference:
(http://en.wikipedia.org/wiki/K%C3%A1roly_Tak%C3%A1cs)

451.

Kim Jong-Il had a director he liked kidnapped from South Korea, put in prison camps for five years until he was "enlightened," and then forced him to make movies, the most famous of them being a pro-communist Godzilla rip-off.

Reference: (https://www.theguardian.com/books/2015/feb/21/kim-jong-il-movie-star-kidnap-plot-north-south-korea-godzilla)

452.

Several ancient cultures believed in the existence of a race of dog headed men called "Cynocephaly".

Reference: (https://en.wikipedia.org/wiki/Cynocephaly)

453.

The French surgeon Serge Voronoff gained fame for his rejuvenation technique of grafting monkey testicle tissue on to the testicles of men.

Reference: (https://en.wikipedia.org/wiki/Serge_Voronoff#Monkey-gland_transplant_work)

454.

The cosmetics company L'Oreal grows approximately five square meters of human skin per year using derma farming. The skin is to be used for pharmaceutical and cosmetic testing.

Reference: (http://www.northjersey.com/news/business/l-oreal-s-plan-to-start-3d-printing-human-skin-1.1337020)

455.

Eminem was so severely bullied in public school that his mother sued the local school board for "failing to sufficiently protect her child."

Reference: (http://thesmokinggun.com/documents/celebrity/it-got-much-better-eminem)

456.

The only time a U.S. Stealth Fighter has ever been shot down was in 1999 in Yugoslavia.

Reference: (https://theaviationist.com/2014/03/27/vega-31-shot-down/)

457.

In addition to long division, which many people learn in elementary school, there is also a version called short division.

Reference: (https://en.wikipedia.org/wiki/Short_division)

458.

Since 1847, the city of San Francisco has licensed people to operate a private police force in a set district. They are the only security patrol allowed in their area.

Reference:
(https://en.wikipedia.org/wiki/San_Francisco_Patrol_Special_Police)

459.

Thomas Jefferson was a cryptographer who invented the wheel cypher, called the Jefferson Disk. This cypher system used a set of wheels or disks, each with the 26 letters of the alphabet arranged around their edge. The system was used by the United States Army from 1923 until 1942.

Reference: (https://en.wikipedia.org/wiki/Jefferson_disk)

460.

Carrie Fischer did so much drugs during her Star Wars years that even John Belushi warned her to slow down.

Reference: (http://www.theguardian.com/film/2010/oct/12/carrie-fisher-cocaine-star-wars?CMP=share_btn_link)

461.

Until 1924, American Indians were not American Citizens.

Reference:(http://www.nebraskastudies.org/0700/frameset_reset.html?http://www.nebraskastudies.org/0700/stories/0701_0146.html)

462.

The "Hindu Milk Miracle" occurred in 1995 when Hindu deity Ganesha allegedly "drank" milk offerings, which led to a media frenzy and massive sale and increase in price of milk. This phenomenon again occurred in 2006.

Reference: (https://en.wikipedia.org/wiki/Hindu_milk_miracle)

463.

In 1999, a guy bought 12,150 servings of pudding, at a cost of $3,140, and in return earned 1,253,000 frequent flyer miles.

Reference:
(https://en.wikipedia.org/wiki/David_Phillips_(entrepreneur))

464.

During windy days, the water in your toilet will move around.

Reference: (http://mentalfloss.com/article/27377/why-does-toilet-water-move-when-its-windy-outside)

465.

In 1994, a FedEx employee attempted to hijack a cargo plane, kill the 3 crew members with claw hammers and a spear gun, and then crash the plane; he also tried to make the entire thing seem accidental. However, the severely injured pilots fought back and made a successful emergency landing while keeping everyone alive.

Reference:
(https://en.wikipedia.org/wiki/Federal_Express_Flight_705)

466.

Nate Horton is the first, and likely to remain only, NHL player to be credited with a goal in an NHL game which he technically did not play.

Reference: (http://grantland.com/the-triangle/the-nhls-five-most-unbreakable-records/)

467.

The rule of thumb for cruise line comfort is generally given as a minimum of 40 tons per passenger.

Reference: (https://en.wikipedia.org/wiki/Panama_Canal#Tolls)

468.

Japanese Buddhists would self-sacrifice by sealing themselves inside a ship boarded-up like a coffin. At sea they either pulled a wooden plug from the hull and drowned or died of thirst or starvation.

Reference: (http://www.atlasobscura.com/articles/the-selfsacrificing-japanese-pilgrims-who-chose-to-be-swallowed-by-the-sea)

469.

In 1971, Michael Caine saw a Maxwell House Coffee commercial featuring the actress Shakira Baksh and became obsessed with her. A friend in advertising told him where she lived and Caine eventually began dating her, and marrying her in 1973. The couple is still married to this day.

Reference: (https://en.wikipedia.org/wiki/Shakira_Caine)

470.

Dale Decker, a 37 year old man from Wisconsin, slipped a disc and now suffers from Persistent Genital Arousal Syndrome. This means that he orgasms 100 times a day. While many believe that it would be a fantastic problem to have, the problem for Dale is that he experiences these crippling orgasms so often that he can barely leave his house.

Reference: (http://nypost.com/2014/09/22/the-living-hell-of-the-man-who-orgasms-100-times-a-day/)

471.

Panda newborn babies are 1/900th the size of their mother.

Reference: (http://www.huffingtonpost.com/2013/08/31/why-are-panda-babies-so-small_n_3844218.html)

472.

Birds have sex during what's called a cloacal.

Reference:(https://en.wikipedia.org/wiki/Cloaca#Birdshttp://birding.about.com/od/Reproduction/a/How-Birds-Mate.htm)

473.

MC Hammer is a minister and he officiated at Corey Feldman's wedding. Between 1997 and 1998, Hammer claimed that he adopted the "M.C." back into his name which now stood for "Man of Christ."

Reference:(https://en.wikipedia.org/wiki/MC_Hammer#Christian_beliefs_and_pastoral_ministry)

474.

Syrian life expectancy has gone from 75.9 to 55.7 during the Civil War.

Reference: (http://www.theguardian.com/world/2015/mar/12/syrias-war-80-in-poverty-life-expectancy-cut-by-20-years-200bn-lost)

475.

Some aboriginal languages have no words for left/right. As a result, instead of ordering a sequence of images showing someone getting older from left to right, like English speakers would, they order them from east to west, regardless of what way they are facing themselves.

Reference: (http://edge.org/conversation/how-does-our-language-shape-the-way-we-think)

476.

Thomas Edison's first patented invention was a vote recorder for Congress. When it was brought to Congress to exhibit to a committee, the committee's chairman said, "If there is any invention on Earth that we don't want down here, that is it."

Reference: (http://edison.rutgers.edu/vote.htm)

477.

Jack Daniels started making his whiskey when he was 13 years old.

Reference: (http://www.tennesseehistory.com/class/JD.htm)

478.

Before "Decimal Day" in 1971, the British Pound was made up of 240 pence.

Reference: (https://en.wikipedia.org/wiki/Decimal_Day#)

479.

Under Armour, an American company, uses a non-American spelling of "armour", not because it has ties to the likes of Canada or the United Kingdom, but because the founder was trying to get a cool toll-free phone number.

Reference: (http://www.businessinsider.com/how-under-armour-got-its-name-2015-6)

480.

Alan Ralsky, a spammer known as the Godfather of Spam, was signed up for junk snail mail by hundreds of Slashdot readers who found his home address. He said, "they've signed me up for every advertising campaign and mailing list there is. These people are out of their minds. They're harassing me."

Reference: (http://cleaninternetcharity.com/2013/06/24/famous-spammers-case-study-alan-m-ralsky/)

481.

Actor Terrence Howard's father once stabbed a man to death in self-defense while waiting in line to see a department store Santa. Terrence, who was two at the time, witnessed the entire thing.

Reference: (https://en.wikipedia.org/wiki/Santa_Line_Slaying)

482.

Some people identify as an amputee and want their limbs cut off.

Reference:
(https://en.wikipedia.org/wiki/Body_integrity_identity_disorder#Description)

483.

Kenny from South Park was actually based on a real child Trey Parker went to school with. Kenny wore an orange parka that made his voice difficult to understand. Trey and the other kids also joked about Kenny "dying", as Kenny skipped school often.

Reference:
(http://southpark.wikia.com/wiki/Kenny_McCormick#Character_Inspiration)

484.

Sawyer Sweeten, who played one of Raymond's twin sons on the show "Everybody Loves Raymond," shot himself in the head in 2015.

Reference: (https://en.wikipedia.org/wiki/Sawyer_Sweeten#Death)

485.

The coagulation of ejaculated human semen is caused by fibrinogen, which is the same protein which causes blood to clot.

Reference: (http://ebm.sagepub.com.sci-hub.io/content/83/4/692.short)

486.

There is an island in the Caribbean, HMS Diamond Rock, which was considered a commissioned ship of the Royal Navy. The "vessel" played an important role during the Napoleonic wars.

Reference: (https://en.wikipedia.org/wiki/Diamond_Rock)

487.

During World War II, when Japanese soldiers charged American troops, they would sometimes scream, "To hell with Babe Ruth."

Reference:
(https://espn.go.com/sportscentury/features/00016451.html)

488.

In June, 1832, an Irish ex-sailor Dennis Collins was convicted of High Treason for throwing stones at King William IV.

Reference: (https://en.wikipedia.org/wiki/Admiral_Duncan_(pub))

489.

The patron saint of migraine sufferers is St. Aspren.

Reference: (https://en.wikipedia.org/wiki/Aspren)

490.

Operation Uranus was a Soviet military offensive to take German troops from the rear in the Battle of Stalingrad.

Reference: (http://russianrulershistory.com/counterattack-in-stalingrad-operation-uranus/)

491.

The Communist Party of Czechoslovakia wanted to build a state-of-the-art subway network with better trains, but the Soviet Union forced them to use their old, inefficient train designs for the benefit of the Soviet Economy.

Reference:
(https://en.wikipedia.org/wiki/Comecon#Ineffective_production)

492.

In 1913, Hitler, Stalin, Trotsky and Freud all lived in the city of Vienna. What's more, Hitler and Trotsky frequented the same Viennese café.

Reference: (http://www.bbc.com/news/magazine-21859771?repost)

493.

Switzerland had a nuclear weapons program.

Reference:(https://en.wikipedia.org/wiki/Switzerland_and_weapons_of_mass_destruction#Swiss_nuclear_program)

494.

In Western Europe in 1750, a female donkey was put on trial for bestiality. She was acquitted after witnesses attest to its virtue and good behavior, and its human co-conspirators were sentenced to death.

Reference: (https://en.wikipedia.org/wiki/Animal_trial)

495.

A man successfully "foreclosed" on a Wells Fargo office because they failed to respond to his letters of inquiry and then ignored his $1,000 small claims judgment.

Reference: (http://consumerist.com/2011/03/03/patrick-rodgers-describes-how-he-foreclosed-on-wells-fargo-step-by-step/)

496.

Jeff Goldblum's son was born on Independence Day.

Reference:
(https://en.wikipedia.org/wiki/Jeff_Goldblum#Personal_life)

497.

England, Wales, and Scotland are part of Great Britain; Great Britain and Northern Ireland make up the United Kingdom; the United Kingdom, Isle of Man, and the two Channel Islands make up the British Islands; and the British Islands plus the Republic of Ireland make up the British Isles.

Reference:
(http://www.quickanddirtytips.com/education/grammar/whats-the-difference-between-england-great-britain-and-the-uk)

498.

In 1834, a 22-year old milkmaid from the Swedish countryside was arrested in Stockholm for disrupting traffic by gathering large crowds with her beauty. Once released, her beauty was so famous that it became a necessity for trendy aristocrats to pay her to display herself in their salons.

Reference: (https://en.wikipedia.org/wiki/Pilt_Carin_Ersdotter)

499.

Basketballs are orange colored because Butler's Coach Hinkle thought that brown balls were difficult to see.

Reference: (https://www.childrensmuseum.org/blog/why-are-basketballs-orange)

500.

Number 4 is considered an unlucky number in China because it is nearly homophonous to the word "death" (pinyin sǐ). In a study of five years' worth of real estate sales in the greater Vancouver area, researchers found that houses in Chinese neighborhoods with an address containing a 4 sold for an average of $8,000 less than their luckier counterparts.

Reference: (http://www.psmag.com/business-economics/fixer-upper-3br-2ba-lucky-address-78912)

501.

In the United States, keeping a feather from a bald eagle can result in a $25,000 fine.

Reference: (https://en.wikipedia.org/wiki/Eagle_feather_law)

502.

Native American warrior Crazy Horse grew to hate white people after witnessing his tribe being attacked by U.S. troops. They had come because his tribe had slaughtered a cow that accidentally wandered into their village.

Reference: (https://en.wikipedia.org/wiki/Crazy_Horse#Visions)

503.

An American proposed that Australia be colonized and designed the first settlement to consist of Americans, Chinese and Islanders.

Reference: (https://en.wikipedia.org/wiki/History_of_Australia_(1788%E2%80%931850)#Colonisation)

504.

Romans used to call Christians atheists because they didn't pay tribute to their gods.

Reference: (http://en.wikipedia.org/wiki/Anti-Christian_policies_in_the_Roman_Empire)

505.

Poon Kim holds the record for surviving adrift in a life raft at 133 days in 1942 - 1943. When he was told that no one had ever survived longer on a raft at sea, he replied, "I hope no one will ever have to break that record."

Reference: (http://en.wikipedia.org/wiki/Poon_Lim)

506.

Super Bowl halftime shows are such big productions because in 1992, Fox aired an episode of In Living Color. The show drew over 22 million viewers away from the Super Bowl and led the league to consider top performers in subsequent years.

Reference: (https://en.wikipedia.org/wiki/Super_Bowl_XXVI)

507.

Bob Marley's "No Woman No Cry" is actually titled "No Woman Nuh Cry". This translates to "No Woman Don't Cry" and it's a comfort song for a woman, not a comfort song for men with no woman.

Reference: (http://en.wikipedia.org/wiki/No_Woman,_No_Cry)

508.

The word "prolly", which is an informal way of saying "probably," originated in the 1940s.

Reference:
(http://www.oxforddictionaries.com/us/definition/american_english/prolly)

509.

When Disney acquired Star Wars, they ensured all their future works would be equal canon with the original movies.

Reference: (https://en.wikipedia.org/wiki/Star_Wars_canon)

510.

The Lacey Acts was amended in 2008 to prevent U.S. companies from purchasing lumber from illegal sources, such as those engaged in illegal deforestation. Gibson Guitar and Lumber Liquidators, and several other companies, have been charged with violating the act.

Reference: (https://en.wikipedia.org/wiki/Lacey_Act_of_1900)

511.

Approximately 62% of Americans have less than $1,000 in their savings accounts and 21% don't even have a savings account.

Reference: (http://www.marketwatch.com/story/most-americans-have-less-than-1000-in-savings-2015-10-06)

512.

Space Mountain was the first ride to cost more than the original 1955 cost in Disneyland.

Reference:
(http://www.hiddenmickeys.org/disneyland/secrets/tomorrow/Space Mountain.html)

513.

In some areas of the U.S. and elsewhere, "Mary", "merry", and "marry" are pronounced differently.

Reference: (http://dialectblog.com/2011/09/21/marry-merry-mary/)

514.

A female serial killer in Ancient Rome was punished for her crimes by being raped by a giraffe.

Reference: (http://books.google.com/books?id=da_fY9EfydsC&pg=PA129&lpg=PA129&dq=the+serial+killer+files+locusta+punished&source=bl&ots=YIz5bMBKtv&sig=L6J51dxVdNCtbS4Fid1Gs-_IKuw&hl=en&sa=X&ei=1xy9T8HQK4XvggeN7bSpDw&redir_esc=y#v=onepage&q&f=false)

515.

Humans have about 100 million neurons, dubbed the "second brain," embedded in the walls of the long tube of our gut, or alimentary canal, running from the esophagus to the anus. This enteric nervous system enables us to "feel" the inner world of our gut and its contents.

Reference: (http://www.scientificamerican.com/article/gut-second-brain/)

516.

After Mark Twain met Helen Keller at a dinner party, he was so impressed with her that he wrote to the wife of Henry H. Rogers, a wealthy oil magnate, pleading with her to convince her husband to support Keller's education. Mr. Rogers agreed and personally paid for her entire education.

Reference: (http://historyofredding.com/epl/twain-keller-exhibit1.htm)

517.

A hybrid cross of the American Bison and a Tibetan Yak is called a "Yakalo" and a hybrid cross with a cattle is called a "Yakow" but are not actively bred due to low survival rates.

Reference: (http://www.hobbyfarms.com/farm-breeds/others-profiles/yak-2.aspx)

518.

The U.K.'s Oscars of Pornography are called the "SHAFTAS."

Reference: (https://en.wikipedia.org/wiki/Soft_and_Hard_Adult_Film_and_Television_Awards)

519.

The National Rifle Association held its convention in an arena that banned guns.

Reference: (http://nashvillepublicradio.org/post/nra-conventioneers-grumble-about-gun-ban-bridgestone-arena-events#stream/0)

520.

The state of Kentucky currently has 4.9 million barrels of bourbon that are aging. This exceeds the state's own population.

Reference: (https://en.wikipedia.org/wiki/Bourbon_whiskey)

521.

The calculator program that comes with Windows is rated E for Everyone by the ESRB.

Reference: (https://www.microsoft.com/en-us/store/apps/windows-calculator/9wzdncrfhvn5)

522.

Da Hong Pao is the most expensive tea in the world; at a cost of $1,025,000 per kilogram.

Reference: (http://en.wikipedia.org/wiki/Da_Hong_Pao)

523.

Idiot, Imbecile and Moron used to be actual medical terms for different levels of mental handicap.

Reference: (http://www.etymonline.com/index.php?term=moron)

524.

Patients who take immunosuppressant drugs have 64 times as many common skin cancer cells as someone who isn't taking the drugs.

Reference: (http://www.skincancer.org/skin-cancer-information/skin-cancer-facts/weakened-immune-system-can-lead-to-skin-cancer)

525.

Most cave paintings were probably made by women. How do we know this? Well, on average, female hands have a ring finger that is shorter than the index finger (whereas in men, it's the other way around), and this difference is believed to have been more pronounced among ancient people. Applying this rule to the hand prints left on cave paintings, scientists have come to the conclusion that nearly three-quarters of them were made by females.

Reference:
(http://news.nationalgeographic.com/news/2013/10/131008-women-handprints-oldest-neolithic-cave-art/)

526.

Ken Peters is a SeaWorld trainer who was attacked near the end of a show in 2006. For about 10 minutes, the whale repeatedly submerged him to the bottom of the tank. He stayed calm during the entire ordeal and used his training to calm the whale enough to be let go. He still works at the same SeaWorld.

Reference:
(https://www.youtube.com/watch?v=RhVbH2NEeLM&feature=yout
u.be)

527.

The first diesel ships were confusing to other captains, as there was no steam exhaust to signify that a ship was moving, causing ships to unintentionally cross paths.

Reference: (https://en.wikipedia.org/wiki/MS_Selandia#cite_ref-
PMR4-22_6-0)

528.

In the last month of World War II in Europe, all German prisoners of war were reclassified as "Disarmed Enemy Forces" to circumvent the Geneva Convention, and thousands died in mass prison camps of starvation, exposure and disease.

Reference:
(https://en.wikipedia.org/wiki/End_of_World_War_II_in_Europe)

529.

Japanese death row inmates aren't told their date of execution. They wake up each day wondering if today may be their last day.

Reference: (http://japanfocus.org/-David-McNeill/2402/article.html)

530.

One of the more common crossword writers for the New York Times, David Steinberg, is 19 years old. He was first published in the New York Times when he was 14.

Reference:
(http://en.wikipedia.org/wiki/David_Steinberg_%28crossword_edito
r%29)

531.

Fecal transplants actually exist and help cure clostridium difficile.

Reference: (http://www.nytimes.com/2013/01/17/health/disgusting-
maybe-but-treatment-works-study-
finds.html?_r=0&module=ArrowsNav&contentCollection=Health&
action=keypress®ion=FixedLeft&pgtype=article)

532.

Nicolas Cage claims to have invented his own acting style, and plans to write a book on it.

Reference:
(http://en.wikipedia.org/wiki/Nicolas_Cage#Acting_style)

533.

Rhianna Pratchett, author Terry Pratchett's daughter, wrote the plots for both Mirror's Edge and the newest Tomb Raider video game, among other A list titles.

Reference:
(https://en.wikipedia.org/wiki/Rhianna_Pratchett#Video_games)

534.

An Olympic rower stopped mid race to let a family of ducks pass. And still won.

Reference:
(http://en.wikipedia.org/wiki/Bobby_Pearce_%28sculler%29)

535.

The Windows XP default desktop wallpaper is a real picture of a real location with no digital enhancements.

Reference: (http://www.nydailynews.com/life-style/bliss-photog-shares-story-famous-windows-xp-image-article-1.1754436)

536.

Nutella was invented during World War II, when an Italian pastry maker mixed hazelnuts into chocolate to extend his chocolate ration.

Reference: (https://tackk.com/History-Of-Nutella)

537.

The red bits that hang off a turkey's beak are called "snoods" and the ones on its neck and throat are called "wattles."

Reference: (http://wild.enature.com/blog/snoods-and-wattles-a-turkeys-story)

538.

The fastest manned airplane ever built was the "North American" X-15, an experimental rocket-powered plane. One test pilot reached 4,519 miles per hour in 1967, a record which still stands. The X-15 could fly so high that 8 pilots technically qualified as astronauts, according to Air Force standards.

Reference: (https://en.wikipedia.org/wiki/North_American_X-15#Fastest_recorded_flights)

539.

Landmines planted on the coasts during the Falklands War accidentally created penguin sanctuaries. The penguins are too light to detonate the mines, so they live and breed safely. The sanctuaries are so popular and profitable that there are efforts to prevent removal of the mines.

Reference: (http://en.wikipedia.org/wiki/Land_mine)

540.

A hummingbird weighs less than a penny.

Reference: (http://animals.mom.me/weight-hummingbird-3660.html)

541.

Silicon Valley uses their own cognitive enhancing drugs called Nootropics that are said to increase short-term memory.

Reference: (http://fusion.net/story/58131/i-tried-silicon-valleys-favorite-brain-enhancing-drugs/)

542.

John Wayne once shot his friend and fellow actor, Ward Bond, in the back with Bond's shotgun. Bond survived the shot; however, when Bond eventually died, he willed the shotgun to Wayne.

Reference:
(https://en.wikipedia.org/wiki/Ward_Bond#Death_and_legacy)

543.

Polar bear liver contains toxically high levels of vitamin A.

Reference: (http://animals.howstuffworks.com/mammals/eat-polar-bear-liver.htm)

544.

Bugs don't breathe or have lungs. They have a network of tubes where air flows and oxygen is simply absorbed.

Reference: (https://askabiologist.asu.edu/how-insects-breathe)

545.

Four teenage girls lied to have an innocent man convicted of murdering a child. After they were found out, they never apologized, claiming that they did it "for a laugh".

Reference:
(https://en.wikipedia.org/wiki/Murder_of_Lesley_Molseed)

546.

Ottoman Sultan Murad IV banned coffee, tobacco & alcohol, making consumption a capital offense. He would patrol the streets himself, personally killing offenders. Murad was a habitual drinker himself and died of cirrhosis.

Reference: (http://en.wikipedia.org/wiki/Murad_IV)

547.

Gordie Howe, also known as "Mr. Hockey," chose to wear his now iconic #9 because players with lower numbers got the bottom bunk in the sleeper train cars used to travel in when he played for the Detroit Red Wings. He was originally #17.

Reference: (http://www2.tsn.ca/bardown/Story.aspx?id=464884)

548.

The schizophrenic artist Bryan Charnley painted self-portraits for years representing his descent into madness, until his suicide in 1991.

Reference: (http://www.bryancharnley.info/self-portraits-2/charnley_self_portrait_series_02/)

549.

Deforestation and forest degradation account for 17% of global greenhouse gas emissions annually, which is more than the entire transportation sector.

Reference: (http://www.ucsusa.org/global_warming/solutions/stop-deforestation/deforestation-global-warming-carbon-emissions.html#.Vm4LeEqDFBd)

550.

Early telephones had no ringers and no hang-up hooks. Callers would get the attention of those they were calling by yelling loudly (often, "ahoy!") into the receiver until someone on the other end noticed.

Reference: (http://blog.summary.com/2012/06/11/the-idea-factory/)

551.

Winona Ryder's father, Michael Horowitz, is the owner of Flashback Books, a mail-order bookselling business that deals in rare printed materials on the history and science of psychoactive drugs.

Reference: (https://en.wikipedia.org/wiki/Michael_Horowitz)

552.

Darth Vader's costume was largely inspired by the Fighting Devil Dogs villain "The Lightning" who also had white Stormtroopers and flew in a triangular ship.

Reference:
(https://en.wikipedia.org/wiki/Star_Wars_sources_and_analogues)

553.

The Atlantic flyingfish can glide up to 12 meters or 39 feet in the air after jumping out of the water.

Reference: (https://en.wikipedia.org/wiki/Atlantic_flyingfish)

554.

An estimated 10,000 cats are eaten per day in China's Guangdong province.

Reference:
(http://www.msnbc.msn.com/id/28292558/#.T70CK8WRUfV)

555.

A study of alcohol-stealing monkeys found that they could be divided into four groups: teetotaler, social drinker (the majority who only drink with other monkeys and not before lunch), regular drinker and binge drinkers that will drink themselves into a coma or death.

Reference: (http://www.theguardian.com/science/punctuated-equilibrium/2011/apr/26/1)

556.

The United States has not ratified the Convention on the Rights of the Child, which protects and promotes the rights of children to survive and thrive, to learn and grow, and to make their voice heard. Somalia and 195 other nations have done so.

Reference: (http://childrightscampaign.org/why-ratify)

557.

Russian voters used to have a box on their ballots to vote for "against all".

Reference: (http://en.wikipedia.org/wiki/Refused_ballot#Russia)

558.

The United States Government forced the residents of Bikini Atoll to move to multiple uninhabitable islands to conduct nuclear testing, moved them back to a radioactive wasteland, and now has them living on a tiny island and off of subsidies.

Reference: (https://en.wikipedia.org/wiki/Bikini_Atoll)

559.

In Ancient China, they used mannequins to lure enemies to shoot arrows, and then they would pull them down and get a free supply of arrows.

Reference: (http://en.wikipedia.org/wiki/Mannequin#Military_use)

560.

4.5% of the land area of the United States is a preserved wilderness area to be, "an area where the Earth and community of life are untrammeled by man, where man himself is a visitor who does not remain."

Reference:
(https://en.wikipedia.org/wiki/National_Wilderness_Preservation_Sy stem)

561.

In 1974, a man stole a helicopter, flew it to Washington, D.C. and hovered for six minutes over the White House before descending on the south lawn. He only spent 1 year in prison and was fined $2,400 for this.

Reference: (http://nymag.com/daily/intelligencer/2014/09/weird-white-house-intruders-security-breeches.html)

562.

In Ancient Egypt, to keep the Nile River's flow stable, Pharaohs were required to masturbate frequently and one of these times had to be done ceremonially in the Nile River.

Reference:
(https://en.wikipedia.org/wiki/History_of_masturbation#Ancient_his tory)

563.

Jeremy Clarkson's fondness for wearing jeans has been blamed by some for the decline in sales of denim in the mid-1990s, particularly Levis.

Reference:
(https://en.wikipedia.org/wiki/Jeremy_Clarkson#Personal_life)

564.

Spree killer, Mark Essex, used a high powered sniper rifle to shoot at policemen while setting up traps and using tactical distractions. He did this because he wanted to wage war against New Orleans. He was so effective in his spree that the U.S. Marine Corps helicopter was loaned to the police so that they could counter attack him while being perched atop a hotel in a fortified position.

Reference:
(http://www.crimelibrary.com/notorious_murders/mass/mark_essex/15.html)

565.

Erasable pens use liquid rubber cement to form lines on paper that can be easily removed for about 10 hours, after which, it hardens and becomes non-erasable.

Reference: (http://home.howstuffworks.com/pen5.htm)

566.

There are 17 American men in history who have run under 2:10 in a marathon. In contrast, there were 32 Kenyans who did it just in October of 2011.

Reference: (http://www.wnyc.org/story/how-one-kenyan-tribe-produces-the-worlds-best-runners/)

567.

Japanese swordsmiths are limited to making 24 per year, which is one of the reasons they cost so much.

Reference: (http://en.wikipedia.org/wiki/Shinken)

568.

Ancient Mesoamericans played a ball game that was basically a mixture of football, racquetball and basketball. In official matches, the losing team was used as human sacrifices.

Reference: (http://www.ancient.eu/article/604/)

569.

Protestors in Thailand adopted the sandwich as a form of protest. Protestors were arrested for, "possession of a sandwich with ill intent."

Reference: (http://www.globalpost.com/dispatch/news/regions/asia-pacific/thailand/140625/four-absurdly-harmless-acts-now-criminalized-thai)

570.

Some inmates in Greenland hold the keys of their own cells. They may leave the premises during the day to go to work or school and they are even allowed to go hunting with rifles.

Reference: (http://www.huffingtonpost.com/2012/01/04/greenland-prison-system_n_1181697.html)

571.

The Russians were the first to photograph the Moon from its surface, but the British saw the photos first.

Reference: (http://www.bbc.co.uk/programmes/p005xg72)

572.

It's illegal for drug companies to advertise to consumers almost everywhere in the world except in the U.S. and New Zealand.

Reference:(https://en.wikipedia.org/wiki/Directtoconsumer_advertising#Nations_permitting_DTC)

573.

The Netherlands has a feral population of rose-ringed parakeets.

Reference: (https://en.wikipedia.org/wiki/Rose-ringed_parakeet#Feral_birds)

574.

There is a persistent storm in Venezuela that produces lightning 140 to 160 nights a year, 10 hours per day and up to 280 times per hour and it's been going since at least the 16th century.

Reference: (http://www.fogonazos.es/2007/06/catatumbo-everlasting-storm.html)

575.

There is a condition in which you think you hear a loud bang as you fall asleep when there's really nothing there. More unsettling than that is the name, Exploding Head Syndrome.

Reference: (http://en.wikipedia.org/wiki/Exploding_head_syndrome)

576.

A 63 year old man traveled from Windsor to Toronto to fulfill a lifelong dream of visiting a Legoland Discovery Center. He was turned away because he didn't have a child with him since Legoland has a policy that requires adults to be accompanied by children.

Reference: (http://www.ctvnews.ca/canada/legoland-dream-dies-for-man-63-over-rule-that-adults-must-be-accompanied-by-kids-1.1358249)

577.

In the very first Grand Theft Auto game, you could choose to play as either a police officer or a robber.

Reference: (http://www.techinsider.io/grand-theft-auto-started-out-as-cops-versus-robbers-2015-4)

578.

In the 1950s, CBS had "Operation Rainbow" where they placed color televisions in stores and other public places to promote color televisions.

Reference: (http://history1900s.about.com/od/1950s/qt/Color-TV.htm)

579.

Leonardo DiCaprio has never done drugs and had to get taught how to play being high by drug experts for his movie roles.

Reference: (http://time.com/5590/leonardo-dicaprio-drugs/)

580.

A fifth wheel was a concept to help with parallel parking in the 1950s.

Reference: (https://www.youtube.com/watch?v=296E57CxNw4)

581.

Calculus means "little stone" from the beads the Romans used on their abacuses.

Reference: (https://en.wikipedia.org/wiki/Roman_abacus)

582.

A Tamil-American scientist Dr. Shiva Ayyadurai created and copyrighted a software called "EMAIL" in 1982. He claims that he is the true inventor of e-mail and that his undergraduate professor, Noam Chomsky, supports his claims.

Reference:(https://en.wikipedia.org/wiki/Shiva_Ayyadurai#Development_of_software_named_.22EMAIL.22_and_controversy_about_its_relation_to_email)

583.

Java, Indonesia is the most crowded and populated island in the world with 130 million inhabitants but still maintains many natural parks and rainforests.

Reference: (http://wikitravel.org/en/Java)

584.

A one of a kind sulfur based ecosystem exists in a Romanian cave completely sealed off from the rest of the world.

Reference:
(http://www.thenakedscientists.com/HTML/content/interviews/interview/1600/)

585.

Cookies came from bakers making small "test cakes" to test the temperature of wood-fired ovens.

Reference:
(http://whatscookingamerica.net/History/CookieHistory.htm)

586.

Edgar Alan Poe was the first person to state that space and time were linked.

Reference: (https://en.wikipedia.org/wiki/Eureka:_A_Prose_Poem)

587.

In 2012, the White House responded to a petition to have a Death Star built by stating that "the Administration does not support blowing up planets" and that it would not fund a weapon "with a fundamental flaw that can be exploited by a one man starship."

Reference:
(http://en.wikipedia.org/wiki/Death_Star#White_House_petition)

588.

Harriet Tubman had her skull sawed off and got brain surgery while awake and biting a bullet after declining anesthesia.

Reference:(https://en.wikipedia.org/wiki/Harriet_Tubman#AME_Zion_Church.2C_illness.2C_and_death)

589.

Google engineers gave serious thought to starting a research project on teleportation.

Reference: (http://bgr.com/2013/05/29/google-teleportation-research-project/)

590.

10% of public school children are enrolled in year-round school systems.

Reference: (http://www.statisticbrain.com/year-round-school-statistics/)

591.

Before breaking the baseball color barrier, Jackie Robinson played semi-professional football in Hawaii, leaving Honolulu on a ship just two days before the attack on Pearl Harbor.

Reference: (https://worldhistoryproject.org/1941/9/1/jackie-robinson-plays-for-the-honolulu-bears)

592.

Charles, the Duke of Orleans, died from a plague because he rolled around in a plague victim's bed, believing that his royal status would protect him.

Reference:
(https://en.wikipedia.org/wiki/Charles_II_de_Valois,_Duke_of_Orl%C3%A9ans)

593.

The International Space Station uses visiting spacecrafts to provide additional boost for keeping it in orbit.

Reference:
(https://en.wikipedia.org/wiki/International_Space_Station#Orbit)

594.

Jägermeister was originally intended to be cough medicine.

Reference:
(http://en.wikipedia.org/wiki/J%C3%A4germeister#History)

595.

In order to be fair to all religions, in addition to Bibles, kids in some Florida schools are also going to have access to literature from their local Satanic Temple.

Reference: (http://twentytwowords.com/heres-the-complete-satanic-activity-book-that-florida-school-children-are-being-given/)

596.

A New York window washer survived a 47 foot fall by using the platform and managed a full recovery right after.

Reference:
(http://www.nytimes.com/2008/01/04/nyregion/04fall.html?pagewanted&_r=0)

597.

The Football Battalion was a fighting unit in World War I, whose core was made up primarily of professional football players. Soldiers came from well-known teams such as Manchester United, Arsenal and Liverpool.

Reference:
(https://en.wikipedia.org/wiki/Football_Battalion#Soldiers)

598.

There was an initiative to create LEGO Age of Empires II sets, but it didn't happen because there weren't enough supporters.

Reference: (https://ideas.lego.com/projects/52276)

599.

Frankincense smoke is psychoactive and incense may act as a weak drug during religious ceremonies.

Reference: (http://www.scientificamerican.com/article/mass-appeal/)

600.

A cave in France has the footprints of an 8- to 10-year-old boy left in the mud 26,000 years ago alongside the paw prints of either a wolf or a large dog; the oldest evidence of human/canine relationships ever found.

Reference:
(http://www.wsj.com/articles/SB10001424052970203554104577001843790269560)

601.

The plastic card where the United States nuclear launch codes are written include codes which have no meaning. The President must memorize where the correct code is located on the list, which allows him to positively identify himself as the Commander-In-Chief and thereby authenticate a launch order.

Reference: (https://en.wikipedia.org/wiki/Gold_Codes)

602.

A German man broke into prison every single night to visit his girlfriend.

Reference: (http://www.spiegel.de/international/zeitgeist/punished-for-love-man-indicted-for-breaking-into-prison-a-678721.html)

603.

A private company trademarked historic places and well-known images in Yosemite National Park, forcing the park to rename many landmarks.

Reference: (http://www.outsideonline.com/2048041/who-owns-yosemite)

604.

No one knows what Jesus looked like; "The artistic depictions down the ages have total and complete variation, which indicates that nobody did a portrait of Jesus or wrote down a description, it's all been forgotten."

Reference: (http://news.bbc.co.uk/2/hi/3958241.stm)

605.

ATM PINs were originally intended to have six digits, but have four because the inventor's wife said she could only remember that many.

Reference: (http://news.bbc.co.uk/2/hi/business/6230194.stm)

606.

The Cuckoo catfish lays its eggs among the eggs of the mouth brooding cichlid fish, which carries its young in its mouth. The catfish eggs hatch first inside the cichlid mother's mouth, then proceed to eat the cichlid eggs present before being released by the cichlid.

Reference: (https://www.youtube.com/watch?v=tnvbVIcZZHc)

607.

Petroleum can be used as a narcotic.

Reference: (http://news.discovery.com/human/health/crude-oil-harms-humans.htm)

608.

270 million years ago, there was a crocodile looking amphibian that measured 9 meters or 30 feet.

Reference: (https://en.wikipedia.org/wiki/Prionosuchus)

609.

Woody Harrelson was arrested for planting 4 hemp seeds in Kentucky as an act of protest.

Reference:
(http://abcnews.go.com/Entertainment/story?id=2969864&page=1)

610.

The Duke of Edinburgh warned Princess Diana that, "if you don't behave, my girl, we'll take your title away." Princess Diana replied with, "My title is a lot older than yours, Philip."

Reference:
(https://en.wikipedia.org/wiki/Diana,_Princess_of_Wales#Divorce)

611.

The "Flitch of Bacon" custom in old England has couples, who had been married for one year and one day, be given a free side of bacon if they swore that they didn't regret their wedding.

Reference:
(https://en.wikipedia.org/wiki/Flitch_of_bacon_custom#Older_tradit
ions)

612.

A woman without a vagina performed oral sex, got in a knife fight, and was impregnated when the sperm passed from her stomach to her uterus.

Reference:
(http://blogs.discovermagazine.com/seriouslyscience/2013/08/09/frid
ay-flashback-thats-one-miraculous-conception/#.VEazmGK9KK0)

613.

As a German college student, Leonie Müller paid roughly $380 dollars a month to live on a train because it was cheaper than paying rent

Reference: (http://www.mnn.com/green-
tech/transportation/blogs/she-lives-train-because-its-cheaper-than-
rent)

614.

A five year old boy was the victim of a ritual human sacrifice, in reaction to the most powerful earthquake recorded.

Reference:
(http://en.wikipedia.org/wiki/1960_Valdivia_earthquake#Human_sa
crifice)

615.

When Perdue Pharmaceuticals made OxyContin crush, melt and tamper resistant in 2010, prescriptions fell 20% nationwide and heroin overdose rose by 20%.

Reference: (http://www.solutions-recovery.com/addiction-info/crush-resistant-oxycontin.html)

616.

Between 94% and 98% of all alarm calls to law enforcement are false alarms.

Reference:
(https://en.wikipedia.org/wiki/Security_alarm#False_and_absent_ala
rms)

617.

Saddam Hussein's grave is currently a toilet.

Reference: (http://www.csmonitor.com/World/Middle-East/2016/0316/Iranian-war-photographers-what-makes-them-click)

618.

You urinate more when you're cold because of an increase in your arterial blood pressure caused by blood being taken away from your extremities and crammed in your core. Your kidneys shed fluid to try and stabilize it.

Reference: (https://en.wikipedia.org/wiki/Diuresis#Cold-induced_diuresis)

619.

A father and son were matched against each other in the National Scrabble Championship. The father won by playing "DEFEATED" as his last word.

Reference: (http://www.upi.com/Odd_News/2010/08/09/Father-son-face-off-at-Scrabble/72561281377594/)

620.

Through 50 years of experimentation investigating the domestication of wolves, scientists in Russia successfully domesticated the Silver Fox; a breed of foxes that behave a lot like dogs.

Reference: (http://en.wikipedia.org/wiki/Domesticated_silver_fox)

621.

Ohio has the highest industrial air pollution in the United States.

Reference: (http://www.worldatlas.com/articles/top-20-most-polluted-states-in-the-us.html)

622.

A playwright invented the lithograph when he was too poor to publish his new play with a traditional printing press.

Reference:(https://en.wikipedia.org/wiki/Alois_Senefelder#Discovery.2C_development_of_lithography)

623.

Kangaroo rats, one of the smallest desert mammals, can survive their entire lives without drinking a drop of water. It urinates a highly concentrated paste in order to conserve and recycle any water it does consume through seeds or insects.

Reference:
(http://stamps.umich.edu/ecoexplorers/sonorandesert/home.aboutsonoran.html)

624.

The Dutch East India Company had the ability to wage war, imprison and execute convicts, negotiate treaties, strike its own coins, and establish colonies.

Reference:
(https://en.wikipedia.org/wiki/Dutch_East_India_Company)

625.

Laura Dekker circumnavigated the world single-handedly, when she was 14 years old.

Reference: (http://en.wikipedia.org/wiki/Laura_Dekker)

626.

Achernar, the 10th brightest star in the night sky, spins so fast that its width is over 1.5 times greater than its pole-to-pole diameter.

Reference: (https://en.wikipedia.org/wiki/Achernar)

627.

Chiropractors are not doctors and are dangerous, a survey by the Stanford University Stroke Center found that within a 2-year period, 56 strokes had occurred within 24 hours after receiving neck manipulation by a chiropractor. One patient died, and 86% were left with permanent impairment.

Reference:
(http://www.quackwatch.com/01QuackeryRelatedTopics/chirostroke.html)

628.

Babies under the age of six months can hold their breath and open their eyes under water, making it look like they can swim.

Reference: (http://www.babycenter.com/404_is-it-true-that-babies-are-born-with-the-ability-to-swim_10313062.bc)

629.

The United States Government began mass surveillance of all Americans within a few days after the September 11th attacks.

Reference:
(https://en.wikipedia.org/wiki/William_Binney_(U.S._intelligence_official))

630.

In Iceland, the phonebook is sorted by first names because everyone's surname is basically their father's first name followed by -son or -dottir.

Reference: (http://travel-wonders.com/2009/09/28/the-icelandic-phonebook-surprise/)

631.

The Nintendo Disk Writer was a proprietary disk-based system where games purchased on disks could be taken to a kiosk and overwritten with a newer commercial game, similar to a CD-RW.

Reference: (http://www.famicomdisksystem.com/)

632.

Larry David inadvertently saved a man from his death row sentence by accidentally filming him during a scene at Dodger Stadium that provided the defendant a solid alibi.

Reference: (http://www.cnn.com/2004/LAW/06/07/larry.david/)

633.

The Fremantle Dockers is an Australian Football club who have never won the Premiership and whose mascot is an anchor.

Reference: (https://en.wikipedia.org/wiki/Fremantle_Football_Club)

634.

The statue of George Washington in Trafalgar Square in London sits on imported soil from the U.S. because Washington claimed "he would never again step foot on English soil".

Reference:
(http://www.inetours.com/England/London/pages/Trafalgar_Sq.html
)

635.

There were 37 sets of brothers serving on board the USS Arizona on December 7th, 1941. Almost all of them were killed in action.

Reference:
([http://www.nps.gov/valr/learn/historyculture/brothersassignedarizon a.htm](http://www.nps.gov/valr/learn/historyculture/brothersassignedarizona.htm))

636.

Stephanie Beatriz, who plays Rosa Diaz in "Brooklyn Nine Nine", got her signature scar on her right eyebrow when she tripped on a LEGO brick.

Reference:
(https://en.wikipedia.org/wiki/Stephanie_Beatriz#Early_life)

637.

Steven Spielberg declined to direct the Harry Potter movies and said, "It's just like withdrawing a billion dollars and putting it into your personal bank account. There's no challenge."

Reference: (http://harrypotter.wikia.com/wiki/Warner_Bros.)

638.

The earliest known use of "google" as a verb on American television was in an episode of Buffy the Vampire Slayer in 2002, when Willow asked Buffy, "Have you googled her yet?"

Reference: (https://en.wikipedia.org/wiki/Google_(verb))

639.

The NFL is the most provincial American sport with 96.5% of the players being born in the United States.

Reference: (http://www.businessinsider.com/chart-international-origins-of-nfl-players-2011-11)

640.

Tom Cruise spent two years learning Japanese and swordplay in preparation for the filming of "The Last Samurai."

Reference: (http://thefilmbox.org/top-10/top-ten-samurai-films/6/)

641.

During the first Moon landing, the average age of NASA controllers was 26 years old.

Reference: (http://www.pbs.org/wgbh/nova/tothemoon/kranz.html)

642.

The Manhattan Project "borrowed" 14,700 tons of silver from the Federal Reserve to make the U235 needed for nuclear weapons.

Reference: (https://solari.com/blog/manhattan-project-use-of-silver/)

643.

In 2011, Norway had a "butter crisis," with an acute shortage of butter which resulted in prices soaring.

Reference: (https://en.wikipedia.org/wiki/Norwegian_butter_crisis)

644.

"Santa Claus" is copyrighted by a British company.

Reference: (http://www.forbes.com/2008/12/10/christmas-legal-lawsuits-biz-media-cx_wp_1210christmas.html)

645.

A nightmare refers to a literal night mare. A "mare" is a demon which gives you bad dreams.

Reference: (http://en.wikipedia.org/wiki/Mare_%28folklore%29)

646.

The average British person will spend a year of their life hung-over.

Reference: (http://www.breakingnews.ie/world/average-british-person-spend-year-of-their-life-hungover-641507.html)

647.

It's possible to "scrub" carbon dioxide out of the air. The captured CO2 can then be used to create low-carbon fuels or stored to eliminate the emissions from the atmosphere.

Reference:
(http://www.canadianmanufacturing.com/technology/canadian-firm-builds-giant-scrubber-to-pull-co2-from-the-air-152497/)

648.

At the end of World War II, among the locations considered for the United Nation's headquarters was the small town of Scituate.

Reference:
(https://en.wikipedia.org/wiki/Chopmist_Hill_Listening_Post#Site_for_the_UN.2C)

649.

The Chupa Chups logo was designed by Salvador Dali.

Reference: (http://www.fastcompany.com/1669224/salvador-dal-s-real-masterpiece-the-logo-for-chupa-chups-lollipops)

650.

An Australian man in London, desperate not to miss his daughter's birthday back home, posted himself to Australia in a crate which he helped design and build. He amazingly survived the three days journey and became a news sensation in 1964.

Reference: (http://www.bbc.co.uk/news/magazine-31700049)

651.

The Massachusetts Berkshires region has its own currency, called the BerkShares.

Reference: (https://en.wikipedia.org/wiki/BerkShares)

652.

When identical twins procreate with another set of identical twins, their offspring are both genetic siblings and social cousins.

Reference:
(http://usatoday30.usatoday.com/tech/columnist/aprilholladay/2006-11-20-twins-dice_x.htm)

653.

A species of monkey is named after a casino.

Reference: (https://en.wikipedia.org/wiki/Madidi_titi)

654.

The moon smells like gunpowder.

Reference: (http://science.nasa.gov/science-news/science-at-nasa/2006/30jan_smellofmoondust/)

655.

The sweat from a man's underarm can help women relax, boost their mood and help regulate their menstrual cycle, if applied to her lips.

Reference: (http://www.upenn.edu/pennnews/news/pheromones-male-perspiration-reduce-womens-tension-alter-hormone-response-regulates-menstrual-c)

656.

After being rejected by 20 publishers, Frank Herbert's 1965 sci - fi classic, Dune, was finally picked up by Chilton Books. The publisher was previously known only for big car repair manuals sold in auto parts stores.

Reference:
(http://en.wikipedia.org/wiki/Dune_%28novel%29#Origins)

657.

The primary language of Madagascar, Malagasy, ultimately originated from Taiwan.

Reference: (https://en.wikipedia.org/wiki/Austronesian_languages)

658.

Vin Diesel has never met his father, and doesn't know what race he is.

Reference: (https://en.wikipedia.org/wiki/Vin_Diesel#Early_life)

659.

The world record for having a ferret in your pants is 5 hours and 30 minutes.

Reference: (http://en.wikipedia.org/wiki/Ferret-legging)

660.

You can travel by train from Singapore to London for $2,126.

Reference: (https://vulcanpost.com/2150/he-travelled-from-singapore-to-london-across-14-countries-by-land-it-only-costs-us2126/)

661.

A cameraman for the television show "COPS" was killed during a shooting incident that involved a robbery suspect.

Reference: (http://www.nytimes.com/2014/08/28/us/police-shooting-kills-crew-member-working-for-reality-show-cops.html?referer=&_r=0)

662.

A French mathematician, the day before his duel, published all his work because he didn't think that he would survive. The next day, he died at the age of 20 from a bullet to his gut.

Reference: (http://www.storyofmathematics.com/19th_galois.html)

663.

There is a scene in a Shakespeare play where a character complains about Jews converting to Christianity, eating non-kosher food, and thereby increasing the price of his beloved bacon.

Reference: (http://nfs.sparknotes.com/merchant/page_154.html)

664.

A New Orleans police officer committed an armed robbery, murdering a uniformed policeman and two employees in the process. One employee hid in the freezer and was spared; the officer returned later to "investigate" the crime and was identified by the survivor as the shooter.

Reference: (http://en.wikipedia.org/wiki/Antoinette_Frank)

665.

There is a sausage restaurant in Regensburg, Germany which is in business for 900 years. That means that they were selling sausages well before the Inca Empire existed and are still serving over 6,000 sausages a day.

Reference:
(http://en.wikipedia.org/wiki/Regensburg_Sausage_Kitchen)

666.

Rob Lytle was the first person to score a touchdown in both the Rose Bowl and the Super Bowl.

Reference:
(https://en.wikipedia.org/wiki/Rob_Lytle#Professional_football)

667.

In the 1970s Intervision Song Contest, the Communist equivalent to Eurovision, viewers would vote by turning on lights at a given moment; power plants would measure the load to help determine the winner.

Reference: (https://en.wikipedia.org/wiki/Intervision_Song_Contest)

668.

Tagalog is the fifth most spoken language in the United States, ranking higher than Vietnamese, Korean, German, Arabic and Russian.

Reference: (http://www.worldatlas.com/articles/the-most-spoken-languages-in-america.html)

669.

Stalin's original name was Josif Djugashvili. In 1913, he began using the pseudonym Stalin, meaning "Man of Steel."

Reference: (http://secondworldwar.co.uk/index.php/ww2-trivia)

670.

A Korean man fell in love and eventually married a pillow with an anime character printed on it.

Reference: (http://metro.co.uk/2010/03/09/man-marries-pillow-154906/)

671.

When drinking through a straw, people usually drink faster than if they were drinking regularly.

Reference:
(http://www.personal.psu.edu/afr3/blogs/SIOW/2011/09/do-you-get-drunk-faster-with-a-straw-1.html)

672.

Soap dates back to 2800 BC. A Babylonian clay tablet was discovered with the recipe, while an Egyptian papyrus mentions soap made with animal and vegetable oils. The word "sapo", meaning soap in Latin, is first mentioned in Natural History by Pliny the Elder.

Reference: (https://en.wikipedia.org/wiki/Soap)

673.

Bose created an electromagnetic suspension that keeps the car level over uneven surfaces and aggressive maneuvers.

Reference:
(http://worldwide.bose.com/axa/en_au/web/suspension_system/page.html)

674.

More people have been diagnosed with mental disorders in the United States than in any other nation on Earth.

Reference: (http://theeconomiccollapseblog.com/archives/40-weird-facts-about-the-united-states-that-are-almost-too-crazy-to-believe)

675.

If you could fold a piece of paper in half 103 times it would be as thick as the observable universe.

Reference: (http://www.sciencealert.com/features/20142007-25891.html)

676.

Banana ketchup is popular in the Philippines.

Reference: (http://en.wikipedia.org/wiki/Banana_ketchup)

677.

The largest unclaimed lottery ticket in the United States was worth $77 million dollars.

Reference:
(https://www.lottosignals.com/magazine/knowledge/lottery-winners-gone-missing-the-biggest-unclaimed-lottery-prizes-13-07-2015)

678.

16 year old Ronda Rousey was a moderator of a Pokémon forum, and her username was mew182.

Reference:
(http://www.sbnation.com/lookit/2014/9/3/6102133/ronda-rousey-pokemon-forum-moderator)

679.

When Johnny Cash realized his record label of 30 years was not properly marketing him, he recorded an intentionally awful song called "Chicken in Black" about his brain being transplanted into a chicken, as a protest. It turned out to be a bigger success than any of his other recent material.

Reference: (https://www.youtube.com/watch?v=y_uM87NTFW4)

680.

Iron Man was created by Stan Lee as a challenge to create a hero that no one should like and force people to like him.

Reference: (https://en.wikipedia.org/wiki/Iron_Man#Premiere)

681.

McDonald's used a chemical in silicone breast implants as an ingredient to make Chicken McNuggets.

Reference: (http://naturalsociety.com/4-fast-food-ingredients-way-worse-than-horsemeat/)

682.

McDonald's used a chemical in silicone breast implants as an ingredient to make Chicken McNuggets.

Reference: (http://naturalsociety.com/4-fast-food-ingredients-way-worse-than-horsemeat/)

683.

A penny made between 1909 and 1982 is worth more if you melt it down than if you spend it, due to the amount of copper in it.

Reference: (http://www.coinflation.com/coins/1909-1982-Lincoln-Cent-Penny-Value.html)

684.

After a video that went viral in 2012 showing a bus monitor getting bullied by students – a Canadian man set up a fundraiser to collect $5,000 for a vacation for her. In the end, they ended up collecting and giving the women over $700,000. She has since retired.

Reference: (http://www.cbsnews.com/news/bullied-bus-monitor-receives-700k-check/)

685.

The crack cocaine industry switched from using measuring cups to stolen beakers and test tubes when Pyrex was sold and no longer used borosilicate glass.

Reference: (http://freakonomics.com/2011/04/28/did-the-sale-of-pyrex-hurt-the-crack-cocaine-industry/)

686.

Gene Simmons and Paul Stanley of "Kiss" own an indoor football team called the Los Angeles Kiss.

Reference: (https://en.wikipedia.org/wiki/Los_Angeles_Kiss)

687.

50.9% of fraud is caught due to someone giving a tip.

Reference: (http://www.acfe.com/rttn-conclusions.aspx)

688.

U.S. Supreme Court Justice Clarence Thomas is not a native English speaker and spoke exclusively the Gullah language until his teens.

Reference:
(http://www.nytimes.com/2007/06/17/books/review/Patterson-t.html?_r=0)

689.

The British Royal Family changed their name to the House of Windsor in 1917 due to anti-German sentiment in Britain during World War II. It was previously called the House of Saxe-Coburg and Gotha.

Reference: (http://didyouknow.org/royals/)

690.

Tom Cruise vandalized the world's tallest building in 2010. During the filming of Mission Impossible 4, he climbed to the top of the Burj Khalifa without safety equipment and etched Katie Holmes' name into the spire.

Reference: (http://www.emirates247.com/entertainment/celebrity-gossip/did-cruise-etch-graffiti-on-the-tip-of-burj-khalifa-2011-12-15-1.432913)

691.

J.P. Morgan has a gem, Morganite, named after him because he was Tiffany & Co.'s best customer.

Reference: (http://www.gemselect.com/other-info/about-morganite.php)

692.

There is a sausage restaurant in Regensburg, Germany, which is in business for 900 years. That means that they were selling sausages well before the Inca Empire existed and are still serving over 6,000 sausages per day.

Reference:
(http://en.wikipedia.org/wiki/Regensburg_Sausage_Kitchen)

693.

The voice actresses for the original Powerpuff Girls were never even contacted for voice acting in the rebooted show, expressing disappointment and describing it as, "a stab in the heart".

Reference: (http://www.cartoonbrew.com/voice-acting/powerpuff-girl-actress-on-being-shut-out-of-reboot-a-stab-in-the-heart-114006.html)

694.

Scientists considered bombing Japanese volcanoes in order to trigger an eruption during World War II.

Reference:(http://books.google.co.uk/books?id=_ykDAAAAMBAJ&lpg=PA103&ots=J0tyx4uhhH&dq=bombing+volcano&pg=PA104&redir_esc=y#v=onepage&q=bombing%20volcano&f=false)

695.

Trains in Japan are so punctual, that if they are even 5 minutes late, the passengers get a formal apology, and most times they'll even get a "delay certificate." Delays that are over an hour will also appear on the news.

Reference: (http://en.wikipedia.org/wiki/Rail_transport_in_Japan)

696.

In 1940, while stopped at a French island in the southern Indian Ocean, German sailor, Bernhard Herrmann, fell from his ship while painting the funnel. He is buried in what is referred to as the most southerly German war grave of World War II.

Reference:
(https://en.wikipedia.org/wiki/German_auxiliary_cruiser_Atlantis)

<h1 style="text-align:center">697.</h1>

Inhabitants of Sulawesi keep their dead around their house after they have died.

Reference:
(http://video.nationalgeographic.com/video/indonesia_corpseliveswithfamily)

<h1 style="text-align:center">698.</h1>

Pakistani officials said that 10 people were convicted of shooting Malala Yousafzai. 8 were secretly acquitted and freed instead of serving 25 year jail terms. 2 are serving life sentences. There is a dispute about whether the 8 were ever really convicted or if more were arrested due to public pressure.

Reference: (http://www.npr.org/sections/thetwo-way/2015/06/05/412211887/pakistan-officials-most-arrested-in-malala-yousafzai-attack-secretly-acquitted)

<h1 style="text-align:center">699.</h1>

Pakistani officials said that 10 people were convicted of shooting Malala Yousafzai. 8 were secretly acquitted and freed instead of serving 25 year jail terms. 2 are serving life sentences. There is a dispute about whether the 8 were ever really convicted or if more were arrested due to public pressure.

Reference: (http://www.npr.org/sections/thetwo-way/2015/06/05/412211887/pakistan-officials-most-arrested-in-malala-yousafzai-attack-secretly-acquitted)

<h1 style="text-align:center">700.</h1>

There was a Japanese man who survived 24 days of cold weather by inadvertently falling into a state of hibernation. When he was found, his temperature dropped to 21 degrees Celsius.

Reference:
(http://www.theguardian.com/world/2006/dec/21/japan.topstories3)

701.

A San Diego park's monorail was named the WGASA Rail Line after managers requested an African sounding name. WGASA is actually an acronym for, "Who Gives A Shit Anyway?"

Reference: (http://www.voiceofsandiego.org/all-narratives/fact/fact-check-wild-animal-parks-naughty-line/)

702.

The word "goodbye" is a contraction of a 16th century phrase, "God be with ye."

Reference: (http://www.merriam-webster.com/dictionary/good%E2%80%93bye)

703.

There's a theory that says that we're born already knowing the rules of grammar.

Reference: (https://en.wikipedia.org/wiki/Universal_Grammar)

704.

When Vladimir the Great was trying to decide on the national religion of Russia in 987, he nearly chose Islam; however, after realizing that Muslims weren't allowed to drink alcohol, he decided on Orthodox Christianity instead.

Reference:(http://books.google.com/books/about/Medieval_Russia_980_1584.html?id=9JHwVtL7qDcC&redir_esc=y)

705.

Google recruits programmers by their search habits.

Reference: (https://thehustle.co/the-secret-google-interview-that-landed-me-a-job)

706.

There is a gigantic swastika made of larch trees that went unnoticed for nearly sixty years.

Reference: (http://en.wikipedia.org/wiki/Forest_swastika)

707.

When researchers told American doctors about a case of a 50 year old man with a heart attack, the doctors were less likely to recommend lifesaving medicine if they were shown a picture of a black patient instead of a white one.

Reference:
(http://www.cnn.com/2009/HEALTH/07/23/doctors.attitude.race.weight/)

708.

The Eurasian beavers were hunted to extinction in parts of Sweden, but have now rebounded so successfully that it's actually causing problems.

Reference: (http://www.earthtouchnews.com/conservation/success-stories/in-sweden-the-beavers-are-back-but-is-that-a-good-thing)

709.

Elvis Presley and Andy Warhol had a foot fetish.

Reference: (https://en.wikipedia.org/wiki/Foot_fetishism)

710.

You can become addicted to nasal spray.

Reference: (http://www.fauquierent.net/afrin.htm)

711.

There are 55 replica Liberty Bells in the United States.

Reference:
(https://en.wikipedia.org/wiki/Liberty_Bell#Legacy_and_commemorations)

712.

92 Senegalese troops died in the Gulf War Coalition, which is second only to United States casualties.

Reference: (https://en.wikipedia.org/wiki/Gulf_War)

713.

A man with Hirschsprung's Disease didn't defecate for 13 years, and died at the age of 29. His colon, which is 7 feet long and weighs 47 pounds, is now on display at the Mütter Museum for medical oddities in Philadelphia.

Reference: (https://www.youtube.com/watch?v=510ThicNP5U)

714.

Some Canadian police departments give out "positive tickets" to thank people for doing something good.

Reference: (http://www.positivetickets.com/about.html)

715.

The emperor penguin can dive to a depth of 1,850 feet. That's deeper than any other bird and deeper than the operational range of most naval submarines.

Reference:
(http://animals.nationalgeographic.com/animals/birds/emperor-penguin/)

716.

It costs $14 for people from visa waiver countries to be approved to visit the United States.

Reference: (https://esta.cbp.dhs.gov/esta/)

717.

The Navy e-Reader Device, for use aboard U.S. Navy Submarines, is pre-loaded with Game of Thrones and Lord of the Rings books.

Reference: (http://en.wikipedia.org/wiki/Navy_eReader_Device)

718.

Tickling can be considered abuse.

Reference: (http://www.handinhandparenting.org/article/tickling-kids-can-do-more-harm-than-good/)

719.

Jason Everman got fired from both Nirvana and Soundgarden, then became an Army Ranger.

Reference:
(http://www.nytimes.com/2013/07/02/magazine/evermans-war.html?_r=0)

720.

Superb fairy-wrens teach their eggs a 'secret password' that the young can sing when they hatch. Those that sing the password get food, and the brood parasite eggs (which don't learn the password) go hungry.

Reference: (http://www.wired.com/2014/06/to-beat-a-parasite-birds-teach-their-young-a-secret-password/)

721.

Jehovah's Witnesses teach that Satan and his demons were cast down to Earth from Heaven 100 years ago. This would mean that the event occurred in 1914.

Reference: (https://en.wikipedia.org/wiki/Jehovah%27s_Witnesses)

722.

Stephen King's lawyers had to buy the van that hit King in 1999 to keep it from appearing on eBay.

Reference: (https://en.wikipedia.org/wiki/Stephen_King)

723.

In a healthy body, urine shifts from being acidic to alkaline throughout the day.

Reference: (http://www.chemcraft.net/acidph2.html)

724.

Vietnamese communist revolutionary, Ho Chi Minh, once worked in the United States as a baker, and later in the United Kingdom as a dish washer.

Reference: (https://en.wikipedia.org/wiki/Ho_Chi_Minh#Early_life)

725.

Margaret Anne Cargill was a philanthropist born into one of the wealthiest families in the world. She gave away more than $200 million during her life, always anonymously, and provided that after her death all her wealth go to charity. In 2011, her assets were liquidated, resulting in a $6 billion dollar donation.

Reference: (http://en.wikipedia.org/wiki/Margaret_Anne_Cargill)

726.

Many personal checks written by Marlon Brando were often never cashed as his signature was usually worth more than the amount on the check.

Reference: (http://classichollywoodcentral.com/?p=1585)

727.

$44 billion worth of gift cards have gone unredeemed since 2008.

Reference: (http://nypost.com/2014/01/26/unused-gift-cards-total-44b-since-2008-study/)

728.

Coyotes are such good swimmers that they have colonized islands off the coast of Massachusetts.

Reference: (http://animals.nationalgeographic.com/animals/mammals/coyote/)

729.

Dr. Phil earned $70 million in 2014, making him the 15th highest earning celebrity.

Reference: (https://en.wikipedia.org/wiki/Phil_McGraw)

730.

In 2009, a Gaza City Zoo replaced zebras, which had died of starvation, with painted donkeys.

Reference: (http://www.nbcnews.com/id/33278616/ns/technology_and_science-science/t/gaza-zoo-replaces-zebras-painted-donkeys/#.VmWtCrgrLRY)

731.

The platypus is such a strange animal that scientists thought the first specimen was a hoax.

Reference: (https://www.washingtonpost.com/news/speaking-of-science/wp/2015/04/01/the-platypus-is-so-weird-that-scientists-thought-the-first-specimen-was-a-hoax/?postshare=6141459511261937&tid=ss_tw)

732.

One of the most sacred shrines in Japan is torn down and rebuilt every 20 years. This has been going on for over 1,000 years, and some records indicate it may have started 2,000 years ago.

Reference: (http://www.smithsonianmag.com/smart-news/this-japanese-shrine-has-been-torn-down-and-rebuilt-every-20-years-for-the-past-millennium-575558/?no-ist)

733.

Around 40% of Vietnamese people have the last name Nguyen.

Reference:
(https://en.wikipedia.org/wiki/List_of_people_with_surname_Nguy%E1%BB%85n)

734.

Whoopi Goldberg choose her stage name, not just as a reference to a Whoopee Cushion, but also because her mother thought "Goldberg" was Jewish-sounding enough to make it in Hollywood.

Reference:
(http://en.wikipedia.org/wiki/Whoopi_Goldberg#Early_life)

735.

Cartoon Network paid the City of Boston $2 million dollars for the "Aqua Teen Hunger Force" bombing scare.

Reference: (http://www.geek.com/news/banned-aqua-teen-hunger-force-boston-episode-leaks-online-1620022/)

736.

Steven Russell escaped from prison by using laxatives to fake the symptoms of AIDS. He then called the prison, posing as a doctor, asking for prisoners interested in an experimental treatment, and volunteered. Once out of Texas, he sent death certificates to the prison stating that he had died.

Reference: (http://en.wikipedia.org/wiki/Steven_Jay_Russell)

737.

In 1941, Harry Truman said, "If we see that Germany is winning we ought to help Russia, and if Russia is winning we ought to help Germany, and that way we let them kill as many as possible."

Reference:
(https://en.wikipedia.org/wiki/Bait_and_bleed#Bloodletting)

738.

The CEO of McDonalds is British.

Reference: (https://en.wikipedia.org/wiki/Steve_Easterbrook)

739.

The Soviet Union had a water computer created in 1928 that was used until the 1980s.

Reference: (http://en.wikipedia.org/wiki/Water_integrator)

740.

The highest observes temperature in the universe was briefly seen at the Large Hadron Collider at CERN. Its magnitude was 7.2 trillion degrees Fahrenheit.

Reference: (http://www.fromquarkstoquasars.com/what-is-the-highest-known-temperature/)

741.

"Assume a can opener", is a catchphrase used to mock economists who base their conclusions on unrealistic assumptions.

Reference: (https://en.wikipedia.org/wiki/Assume_a_can_opener)

742.

There was a relatively popular band in the 1980s and 1990s called Holy Soldier, which played Christian Glam Metal.

Reference: (https://en.wikipedia.org/wiki/Holy_Soldier)

743.

A woman's history of vaginal orgasms is discernible from her walk.

Reference: (http://www.ncbi.nlm.nih.gov/m/pubmed/18637995/)

744.

The rock at the summit of Mount Everest is marine limestone and would have been deposited on the seafloor around 450 million years ago.

Reference: (http://www.tulane.edu/~sanelson/eens1110/deform.htm)

745.

ABC News interrupted regular scheduled programming to announce the reintroduction of Coke Classic in 1985.

Reference: (http://en.wikipedia.org/wiki/New_Coke#Reversal)

746.

John Lennon originally wanted Hitler and Jesus Christ on the cover of Sgt. Pepper's Lonely Hearts Club Band.

Reference:(https://en.wikipedia.org/wiki/Sgt._Pepper%27s_Lonely_Hearts_Club_Band#Cover_artwork)

747.

In 2009, during a bar fight in Dublin, a man had his hand cut off with a samurai sword. He proceeded to punch his attacker in the face with the stump.

Reference: (http://www.independent.ie/irish-news/courts/sword-attacker-sliced-off-victims-left-hand-26523796.html)

748.

Rats "laugh" when tickled.

Reference: (https://www.newscientist.com/article/dn25312-do-animals-have-a-sense-of-humour/)

749.

According to a recent survey, a third of millennials that have student debt would sell an organ to get rid of it. The average student debt for students in the United States among last year's class of graduates was just over $35,000; whereas a human organ can go for upwards of $100,000 on the black market.

Reference: (http://www.vice.com/read/a-third-of-millennials-would-give-up-an-organ-to-pay-off-their-student-loans-vgtrn-265)

750.

American flags made in China are banned in the U.S. Military.

Reference: (http://www.businessinsider.com/american-flags-china-2014-2)

751.

Streptococcus mitis, a species of bacteria, survived on the moon for nearly three years.

Reference:
(https://en.wikipedia.org/wiki/Reports_of_Streptococcus_mitis_on_the_Moon)

752.

Andy Warhol had 26 cats and named all of them Sam, except for one that he named Hester.

Reference:
(https://en.wikipedia.org/wiki/25_Cats_Name_Sam_and_One_Blue_Pussy)

753.

There was a Spider-Man movie planned in the 1980's that had Peter Parker turn into, "a hairy, suicidal, eight-armed human tarantula." Stan Lee was unhappy with the treatment of his character and protested until they rewrote the script.

Reference: (https://en.wikipedia.org/wiki/Spider-Man_in_film#Cannon_Films)

754.

Stray dogs in Moscow have mastered the Metro system in search of food.

Reference: (http://www.digitaljournal.com/article/277599)

755.

A bilingual individual can be dyslexic in one language and not the other.

Reference:(http://www.naldic.org.uk/Resources/NALDIC/Initial%20 Teacher%20Education/Documents/Dyslexiaandmultilingualism.pdf)

756.

The French mathematician, Abraham de Moivre, predicted the date of his own death by noticing he slept an extra 15 minutes each day.

Reference: (https://en.wikipedia.org/wiki/Abraham_de_Moivre)

757.

Sikh Gurdawars offer a free meal to all visitors regardless of religion or beliefs.

Reference: (https://en.wikipedia.org/wiki/Langar_(Sikhism))

758.

In 1935, Congress declared war on soil erosion and enlisted kudzu as a primary weapon. More than 70 million kudzu seedlings were grown in nurseries by the newly created Soil Conservation Service.

Reference: (http://www.smithsonianmag.com/science-nature/true-story-kudzu-vine-ate-south-180956325/?no-ist)

759.

Native Americans did not receive U.S. citizenship until 1924.

Reference: (http://en.wikipedia.org/wiki/Indian_Citizenship_Act)

760.

If you were to drink a large amount of coffee all at once, water intoxication would kill you long before a caffeine overdose would.

Reference: (http://scienceblogs.com/worldsfair/2009/05/01/lethal-doses-and-substance-abu/)

761.

All of Roosevelt's speechwriters were out of town the weekend around the Pearl Harbor attack, therefore, he was left alone to draft what was going to be the most important speech of his presidency.

Reference:
(http://www.nytimes.com/2011/12/07/arts/television/pearl-harbor-24-hours-after-on-history-review.html?_r=0)

762.

A man successfully "foreclosed" on a Wells Fargo office because they failed to respond to his letters of inquiry and then ignored his $1,000 small claims judgment.

Reference: (http://consumerist.com/2011/03/03/patrick-rodgers-describes-how-he-foreclosed-on-wells-fargo-step-by-step/)

763.

In June, 1991, the New York Times first wrote about Stratton Oakmont, the firm made famous by the Wolf of Wallstreet, for being under investigation by the Securities and Exchange Commission.

Reference: (http://www.nytimes.com/1991/06/30/business/wall-street-digging-for-details-in-a-prospectus.html)

764.

Since 2011, a 60 year old Australian man has been paid by local councils in Sydney to have sex with prostitutes in illegal brothels in order to gather evidence, so that they can be shut down.

Reference: (http://www.smh.com.au/nsw/this-man-has-had-sex-with-60-prostitutes-8211-and-sydneys-ratepayers-footed-the-bill-20140920-10iwug.html)

765.

Norway had to close a tunnel because it was full of burning cheese.

Reference: (http://www.bbc.com/news/world-europe-21141244)

766.

The United States Navy has developed a railgun that can shoot a 7 pound projectile at a speed of 1.5 miles per second.

Reference: (https://en.wikipedia.org/wiki/Railgun#History)

767.

The flag of Mozambique has an AK-47 on it. This makes it the only flag in the world to have a modern rifle on it.

Reference: (https://en.wikipedia.org/wiki/Flag_of_Mozambique)

768.

Olive oil fraud, also known as adulteration, has been a major issue in recent years, with 400 Italian police officers arresting 23 people and confiscating 85 farms in "Operation Garden Oil."

Reference: (https://en.wikipedia.org/wiki/Olive_oil#Adulteration)

769.

Las Vegas casino manager, Carl Cohen, became a local folk hero after he knocked the caps off Frank Sinatra's front teeth.

Reference:
(https://en.wikipedia.org/wiki/Carl_Cohen_(businessman))

770.

Daniel Norris, a 21 year old baseball player who recently joined the Toronto Blue Jays with a $2,000,000 signing bonus, lives and sleeps in a VW bus. He has also never drank alcohol, works part time in the off-season at a retail store, and spends no more than $800 a month.

Reference: (http://www.grindtv.com/lifestyle/culture/post/meet-pro-baseball-player-lives-van/)

771.

Mad Max: Fury Road wrapped filming with 6,000 hours of raw footage. Margaret Sixel had to work 10 hours a day, 6 days a week, for two years to create the finished product. It took her three months simply to view all of the footage.

Reference:
(https://en.wikipedia.org/wiki/Margaret_Sixel#Mad_Max:_Fury_Road_.282015.29)

772.

In Spanish, the capitalized term "El Nino" refers to the Christ child, so named because periodic warming in the Pacific near South America is often noticed around Christmas.

Reference: (https://en.wikipedia.org/wiki/El_Ni%C3%B1o)

773.

In 2010, a Polish man living in Germany asked doctors to remove what he thought was a several-year old cyst at the back of his head. However, doctors found that the "cyst" was actually a .22-caliber round lodged in his scalp. He didn't noticed it because he was drunk when it happened 5 years ago.

Reference: (http://www.bbc.com/news/world-europe-11078116)

774.

Stephen Fry claims that Douglas Adams told him why he chose the number 42, and that he will take the secret to his grave.

Reference:(http://en.wikipedia.org/wiki/Phrases_from_The_Hitchhiker%27s_Guide_to_the_Galaxy#The_number_42)

775.

There is an American military cemetery in Margraten, Netherlands. On Memorial Day each year, every last grave is "adopted" by a Dutch family that lays flowers over the site.

Reference:
(http://www.spangdahlem.af.mil/news/story.asp?id=123412405)

776.

Switzerland banned nearly all forms of motor-racing after the tragic 1955 Le Mans disaster, where fragments of a crashed car flew into the stands, killing 83 spectators; this is the most deadly accident in motorsport history. Despite numerous attempts to lift it, the ban is still in place to this day.

Reference: (https://en.wikipedia.org/wiki/Sport_in_Switzerland)

777.

Red states are the most dependent on federal funds.

Reference: (https://wallethub.com/edu/states-most-least-dependent-on-the-federal-government/2700/#)

778.

The Merck Manual, the bestselling medical textbook in the world, categorizes flatulence into four categories: the "sliders," the open sphincter, the staccato or drumbeat, and the "bark."

Reference:
(http://www.merckmanuals.com/professional/gastrointestinal-disorders/symptoms-of-gi-disorders/gas-related-complaints)

779.

In Japan, they have lactation bars offering human breast milk. 2,000 ($18 USD) yen gets you a shot and 5,000 ($46 USD) yen gets you the nipple.

Reference: (http://www.tokyoreporter.com/2009/08/06/lactating-ladies-nurse-customers-at-kabukicho-milk-bar/)

780.

Brazil nuts are 1,000 times more radioactive than other foods, and if you took a handful into a nuclear power plant, it is likely to set off the radiation leak alarm.

Reference:
(https://www.youtube.com/watch?v=Dab_LLxpxSg&feature=youtu.be&t=2507)

781.

The Corolla Spider uses quartz crystals to set traps and catch its prey.

Reference:
(https://www.youtube.com/watch?v=LhoRAjUBttM&feature=youtu.be)

782.

The ATF considers smokers who cross a state line to purchase cheaper cigarettes "casual smugglers."

Reference: (https://www.atf.gov/news/pr/tobacco-enforcement)

783.

Ozzy Osbourne's wife, Sharon, encouraged people to sabotage Iron Maiden's last performance of Ozzfest. This included messing with the PA, sabotaging the stage, and throwing eggs at the band.

Reference:
(https://en.wikipedia.org/wiki/Bruce_Dickinson#Ozzfest_incident)

784.

After Hitler ordered the deportation of Denmark's Jewish population, Danish citizens organized a massive evacuation of the Jews to neutral Sweden, despite the risks. In the end, 99% of Danish Jews survived the Holocaust.

Reference:
(http://en.wikipedia.org/wiki/Rescue_of_the_Danish_Jews)

785.

Toilet paper companies have made the paper roughly 20% smaller than they used to be, and have made the cardboard tube larger, all while increasing the price.

Reference: (http://www.npr.org/2015/01/28/382218337/yes-your-toilet-paper-squares-and-rolls-are-shrinking)

786.

Children with gray hair might have a B-12 deficiency.

Reference: (http://www.drgreene.com/qa-articles/children-gray-hair/)

787.

Early telephones had no ringers and no hang-up hooks. Callers would get the attention of those they were calling by yelling loudly (often, "ahoy!") into the receiver until someone on the other end noticed.

Reference: (http://blog.summary.com/2012/06/11/the-idea-factory/)

788.

In 2013, surgeons used Super Glue to mend a baby's brain.

Reference: (http://vitals.nbcnews.com/_news/2013/06/11/18902662-sticky-fix-surgeons-using-super-glue-to-mend-babys-brain?lite)

789.

The atmosphere is so dense on Venus that if you would try to move your arm quickly, you would feel resistance and would almost feel like being in water.

Reference: (http://www.space.com/28357-how-to-live-on-venus.html)

790.

There is a site that offers a fake internet girlfriend service for $250 a month. This includes setting up a profile on a social networking site like Facebook to publicly communicate with you, making up to 2 public phone calls and getting about 10 text messages.

Reference: (http://www.fakeinternetgirlfriend.com/)

791.

Megacities account for 6.7% of the global population but only 3% of the world's water usage.

Reference: (http://arstechnica.com/science/2015/05/megacities-demand-lots-of-energy-but-result-in-lots-of-gdp/)

792.

In the Queen song, "One Vision", the last two words of the lyrics officially claim to be "one vision." However, in the actual song, the last two words Freddie Mercury says is "Fried Chicken."

Reference:
(https://en.wikipedia.org/wiki/One_Vision#.22Fried_chicken.22)

793.

The American Family Association launched a petition to stop the show Lucifer from airing. They said it, "will glorify Satan as a caring, likable person in human flesh."

Reference: (https://en.wikipedia.org/wiki/Lucifer_(TV_series))

794.

While "Stop" signs in France are in English, in Quebec, Canada, they are in French.

Reference:
(http://commons.wikimedia.org/wiki/Stop#Stop_signs_around_the_world)

795.

A species of squid has been observed to leap from the ocean and use pressurized water jets to achieve flight, going as far as 98 feet.

Reference: (http://io9.com/5983316/marine-biologists-confirm-squid-can-fly---ready)

796.

Of the individuals elected as President of the United States, four died in office of natural causes and four were assassinated.

Reference:
(https://en.wikipedia.org/wiki/List_of_Presidents_of_the_United_States)

797.

You burn 650 calories donating one pint of blood.

Reference: (http://www.sott.net/article/262305-Why-donating-blood-is-good-for-your-health)

798.

AT&T used to send bills to iPhone owners that listed every time data was transferred. This resulted in bills being delivered in boxes.

Reference: (https://en.wikipedia.org/wiki/300-page_iPhone_bill)

799.

The pangolin is the world's most trafficked mammal.

Reference: (http://www.iata.org/pressroom/media-kit/Documents/wildlife-presentation-gmd15.pdf)

800.

Recently, some people at the New York Public Library discovered a box containing old reference questions from the 1940s to 1980s. They're posting the questions to their Instagram account, noting, "we were Google before Google existed."

Reference: (http://instagram.com/nypl/)

801.

A fitness trainer intentionally gained over 70 pounds in order to better understand the plight of his overweight clients. He lost all of it six months later.

Reference: (http://edition.cnn.com/2012/06/05/health/drew-manning-fit2fat2fit-lessons/)

802.

All 24 GPS satellites are equipped with atomic clocks that are capable of getting the time stamp to a location to the 100 billionth of a second.

Reference: (http://royal.pingdom.com/2010/03/23/everything-you-ever-wanted-to-know-about-gps/)

803.

The iconic, "Do you know where you are? You're in the jungle baby!", line was actually yelled at Axl Rose by a homeless man in New York.

Reference: (https://en.wikipedia.org/wiki/Welcome_to_the_Jungle)

804.

A worm's mind has been mapped, replicated, and placed inside a Lego robot.

Reference: (http://www.smithsonianmag.com/smart-news/weve-put-worms-mind-lego-robot-body-180953399/?no-ist)

805.

Fox owns the distribution rights for Star Wars episodes 1 to 3, 5 and 6 until 2020. However, they own Episode 4 forever.

Reference:
(http://starwars.wikia.com/wiki/Twentieth_Century_Fox_Film_Corporation)

806.

When McDonald's cut the price of the Big Mac by 75% in 1997 when bought with fries and a drink, the sales actually dropped because consumers were "confused".

Reference:
(http://online.wsj.com/news/articles/SB863127945921198000)

807.

In 1955, the United States Government dropped over 300,000 mosquitoes over the state of Georgia for research purposes.

Reference: (https://en.wikipedia.org/wiki/Operation_Big_Buzz)

808.

In the last years of her life, Rosa Parks became too ill to manage her own financial affairs. When her rent became delinquent, her apartment's ownership company announced that they would let her live rent free in the building for the remainder of her life.

Reference: (http://www.nbcnews.com/id/6659487/)

809.

Stalin's granddaughter runs a boutique in Portland.

Reference:(http://www.oregonlive.com/portland/index.ssf/2011/11/portland_granddaughter_of_jose.html)

810.

Speakers and microphones are the exact same thing but reversed and you can make a microphone from any speaker and vice-versa.

Reference: (http://www.themarysue.com/headphones-as-microphones/)

811.

Before they have mature feathers, young birds have sensitive "pin feathers." They preen to remove wax from the pin feathers so the feathery parts can unfold.

Reference: (https://en.wikipedia.org/wiki/Pin_feather)

812.

The brain of London cab drivers undergo large structural changes because of the massive amount of knowledge they must memorize.

Reference:
(http://onlinelibrary.wiley.com/doi/10.1002/hipo.20233/abstract)

813.

Ronald Reagan, while on his first presidential trip to the Soviet Union in May, 1988, carried a gun in his briefcase.

Reference:
(http://www.ontheissues.org/Celeb/Ronald_Reagan_Gun_Control.ht

m)

814.

Russia's Vladimir Putin brought a large dog with him to a round of negotiations with Germany's Angela Merkel, knowing that she had a pathological fear of dogs, in order to gain a psychological edge.

Reference: (http://www.psychologytoday.com/blog/canine-corner/200904/vladimir-putin-and-his-political-dog)

815.

A tick bite can cause a lifetime allergy to red meat. The Lone Star tick injects a type of sugar found in red meat into the blood, and causes antibodies to be made that cause an allergic reaction when the person later ingests meat with the sugar.

Reference: (http://www.newyorker.com/tech/elements/can-ticks-make-you-allergic-to-red-meat)

816.

Doctors in the eleventh century would drink the urine of their patients to determine whether or not they had diabetes. A sugary taste indicated the person was diabetic.

Reference: (http://www.defeatdiabetes.org/diabetes-history/)

817.

Parents of the missing Beaumont children received letters from their "captor" agreeing to return them. He never showed and 24 years later, the letters were found to be fake. The author had written them as a joke but was never charged.

Reference:
(https://en.wikipedia.org/wiki/Beaumont_children_disappearance#False_letters)

818.

When the recipe for clam dip first aired on television on the Kraft Music Hall show in the early 1950s, New York City sold out of canned clams within 24 hours.

Reference: (https://en.wikipedia.org/wiki/Clam_dip)

819.

Gas companies in Massachusetts aren't required to fix "nonexplosive" natural gas leaks, and 20,000 ongoing leaks exist, dating back to 1985.

Reference: (http://www.heetma.org/squeaky-leak/natural-gas-leaks-maps/)

820.

Texas cancelled its last meal program after an inmate ordered two chicken fried steaks, a triple-meat bacon cheeseburger, a large bowl of fried okra, a pound of barbecue, three fajitas, a meat lover's pizza, a pint of ice cream, and a slab of peanut butter fudge and didn't eat any of it.

Reference:
(https://en.wikipedia.org/wiki/Murder_of_James_Byrd_Jr.#Last_meal)

821.

Kenya gets 65.8% of its electricity from renewable sources.

Reference:
(https://en.wikipedia.org/wiki/Renewable_energy_in_Kenya)

822.

In the 2011 Tohoku Earthquake, residents of Sendai received 10 to 30 second warnings while Tokyo received a 60 second warning from

Japan's Earthquake Early Warning system before the major seismic waves hit.

Reference: (http://spectrum.ieee.org/tech-talk/computing/networks/japans-earthquake-earlywarning-system-worked)

823.

The sex trade spikes during Democratic and Republican Conventions.

Reference: (http://abcnews.go.com/Blotter/story?id=5629167)

824.

90% of luxury purchases, which some analysts say is a $300 billion dollar industry, still happen in retail stores.

Reference: (http://www.bloomberg.com/bw/articles/2014-04-03/luxury-brands-should-sell-their-products-online)

825.

A researcher found that it takes no more than 3.5% of the population of a country participating in sustained nonviolent civil disobedience to topple a totalitarian government.

Reference: (http://www.washingtonpost.com/blogs/worldviews/wp/2013/11/05/peaceful-protest-is-much-more-effective-than-violence-in-toppling-dictators/)

826.

In 2004, the FBI warned of a mortgage fraud epidemic.

Reference: (http://www.cnn.com/2004/LAW/09/17/mortgage.fraud/)

827.

In Oslo, Norway, there is a free medical clinic for undocumented immigrants. They will even provide patients with a translator at no charge.

Reference: (http://www.bymisjon.no/Virksomheter/Helsesenteret-for-papirlose-migranter/English/)

828.

Albert Einstein claimed that, "compound interest is the eighth wonder of the world."

Reference: (http://www.goodreads.com/quotes/76863-compound-interest-is-the-eighth-wonder-of-the-world-he)

829.

The first Soviet infrared air-to-air missile was copied from a Sidewinder that got stuck in a MiG's wing.

Reference: (https://en.wikipedia.org/wiki/K-13_(missile)#Background_-_the_Sidewinder_missile)

830.

In the early centuries of the Islamic Caliphate, Islamic law allowed citizens to freely express their views, including criticism of Islam and religious authorities, without fear of persecution.

Reference: (https://en.wikipedia.org/wiki/Criticism_of_Islam?oldformat=true#Medieval_world)

831.

Richard Stanley was fired from the making of "The Island of Dr. Moreau." According to the Lost Souls documentary, Stanley came back disguised as an extra on the movie he had been hired to direct.

Reference:
(https://en.wikipedia.org/wiki/The_Island_of_Dr._Moreau_(1996_film))

832.

During the Gulf War, a trench network filled with Iraqi soldiers was in the way of the U.S. military, so they used armor plated bulldozers to pave the trenches over.

Reference:
(https://en.wikipedia.org/wiki/Gulf_War#Bulldozer_assault)

833.

A study by researchers published in The Lancet, scrutinized deaths between 1990 and 2001 of residents of three Siberian industrial towns with typical mortality rates and determined that 52% of deaths of people between the ages of 15 and 54 were the result of alcohol abuse.

Reference:
(https://www.wikipedia.org/wiki/Alcohol_consumption_in_Russia)

834.

There was an octopus who figured out how to short circuit a light in its aquarium.

Reference:
(http://www.telegraph.co.uk/news/newstopics/howaboutthat/3328480/Otto-the-octopus-wrecks-havoc.html)

835.

In 2000, a pediatrician was driven from her home in Wales when local vigilantes confused her job title with "pedophile."

Reference:
(http://www.theguardian.com/uk/2000/aug/30/childprotection.society)

836.

75% of Japanese homes have a hi-tech toilet and the latest models eliminate the need for toilet paper, keep you warm, check your blood pressure, play running-water sounds to increase privacy and open and close automatically so you don't have to touch anything.

Reference: (http://www.nydailynews.com/news/national/new-high-tech-toilets-not-require-hands-paper-article-1.1710437)

837.

During the Gulf War, a trench network filled with Iraqi soldiers was in the way of the U.S. military, so they used armor plated bulldozers to pave the trenches over.

Reference:
(https://en.wikipedia.org/wiki/Gulf_War#Bulldozer_assault)

838.

The Tetris theme song is actually a 19th century Russian folk song called "Korobeiniki."

Reference: (https://en.wikipedia.org/wiki/Korobeiniki)

839.

Machine guns mounted on early propeller aircraft had to be timed to fire bullets through the spinning blades without hitting them.

Reference: (http://en.wikipedia.org/wiki/Synchronization_gear)

840.

Dennis Wilson, the only member of the Beach Boys who could actually surf, died by drowning.

Reference:
(http://en.wikipedia.org/wiki/Dennis_Wilson#Charles_Manson)

841.

The first gold medal that Australia ever won in the Winter Olympics was in short track speed skating. Steven Bradbury won because the four people ahead of him in the finals all crashed and fell in the last curve.

Reference: (https://www.youtube.com/watch?v=fAADWfJO2qM)

842.

The state of Kentucky currently has 4.9 million barrels of bourbon that are aging. This exceeds the state's own population.

Reference: (https://en.wikipedia.org/wiki/Bourbon_whiskey)

843.

IKEA's headquarters are in the Netherlands and not Sweden.

Reference: (https://en.wikipedia.org/wiki/IKEA)

844.

FedEx uses several empty cargo planes that roam the country's skies overnight in circuitous flight paths, ready to divert on demand in order to accommodate unexpected package volume.

Reference:
(http://www.utsandiego.com/uniontrib/20051013/news_1b13fedex.html)

845.

US Marine, John Kelly, was the last person to be awarded 2 Medals of Honor. He ran 100 yards in advance of the front line and attacked an enemy machine gun nest, killed the gunner with a grenade, shot another man with his pistol, and returned with 8 prisoners. He was 19.

Reference: (http://en.wikipedia.org/wiki/John_J._Kelly)

846.

The International Space Station has an espresso machine to simulate the comforts of home.

Reference:
(http://www.nasa.gov/mission_pages/station/research/experiments/1769.html)

847.

Sir Anthony Hopkins was a musician and composer.

Reference: (http://qpolitical.com/after-weeks-of-rumors-anthony-hopkins-just-posted-shocking-news/)

848.

Because they were forgotten about during the Treaty of Versailles, Andorra remained legally in World War I until 1958, when they made peace with Germany.

Reference:
(https://en.wikipedia.org/wiki/History_of_Andorra#20th_century)

849.

People get shorter throughout the day as the water within the intervertebral disks are squeezed out during standing and movement. This water is reabsorbed during sleep when lying down. The average person is 2 centimeters taller in the morning that he is at the end of the day.

Reference:
(http://kidshealth.org/kid/grownup/getting_older/shrink.html)

850.

Humans can live unprotected in space for about 30 seconds if they don't hold their breath.

Reference:
(http://imagine.gsfc.nasa.gov/ask_astro/space_travel.html)

851.

In 2011, a man killed his wife inside the Wal-Mart she was working at. Rather than close the store, they chose to just rope off the gore splattered area while police investigated.

Reference: (http://nydailynews.com/news/national/cops-man-stabs-wife-death-bank-south-carolina-walmart-article-1.991478)

852.

The founder of McDonald's has a Bachelor degree in Hamburgerology.

Reference: (http://en.wikipedia.org/wiki/Hamburger_University)

853.

Water fog sprayed around the vehicle can absorb radars in the 94 GHz band.

Reference:
(https://en.wikipedia.org/wiki/Smoke_screen#Infrared_smokes)

854.

There is a spider that turns into a "wheel" and cartwheels away when it is in danger.

Reference: (https://www.youtube.com/watch?v=V4odlo0Afjs)

855.

Tasmania woodchopper, David Foster, was the first person in any sport to win 1000 Championships. He is also the winner of 178 World Titles and 168 Australian Titles. He weighs 350 pounds or 158 kilograms and he can chop a 12 foot log in 8 seconds.

Reference: (http://www.celebrityspeakers.com.au/david-foster/)

856.

Getting the wind knocked out of you feels like suffocating because it results in temporary paralysis of the diaphragm, inhibiting its function in the breathing cycle.

Reference:
(https://en.wikipedia.org/wiki/Getting_the_wind_knocked_out_of_you)

857.

Cape Coral, a master planned city in South Florida with a population of 154,000 people in an area of 120 square miles, has over 400 miles of canals, which is more than any other city in the world.

Reference: (https://en.wikipedia.org/wiki/Cape_Coral,_Florida)

858.

One of the sons of Frank Herbert, author of Dune, was a gay rights activist who died of AIDS in 1993.

Reference: (https://www.qbd.com.au/brian-herbert/)

859.

The Earth gets a 100 tons heavier every day due to falling space dust.

Reference: (http://science.nasa.gov/science-news/science-at-nasa/2011/01mar_meteornetwork/)

860.

During the construction of One World Trade Center, the steel skeleton was temporarily stabilized by shipping containers which housed break rooms, bathrooms and even a fully functioning Subway.

Reference: (https://www.youtube.com/watch?v=-9FnJCMtOYs&feature=youtu.be&t=34m14s)

861.

The inventor of the windshield wiper, Mary Anderson, was granted a patent for it in 1903, she tried to sell the rights in 1905 and was told that it held no commercial value and was unable to sell it. 19 years later, they became standard equipment on every vehicle.

Reference:
(https://en.wikipedia.org/wiki/Mary_Anderson_(inventor))

862.

The meaning of "red herring" comes from the use of pickled fish as a distraction while training hunting dogs.

Reference:
(https://en.wikipedia.org/wiki/Red_herring#History_of_the_idiom)

863.

Pokémon was banned in Saudi Arabia.

Reference:
(https://en.wikipedia.org/wiki/Pok%C3%A9mon#Morality_and_religious_beliefs)

864.

A man named Walter Summerford was struck by lightning 3 times in his life. After his death, his gravestone was also struck.

Reference: (http://www.scientificamerican.com/article/statistician-david-j-hand-shows-how-the-seemingly-improbable-becomes-a-sure-thing/)

865.

During prohibition, a jury that had heard a bootlegging case was itself put on trial after it drank the evidence. They said they did it to determine whether or not it contained alcohol.

Reference: (http://en.wikipedia.org/wiki/10_Things_You_Don%27t_Know_Ab out)

866.

Around 1,000 homeless people live in flood tunnels under Las Vegas.

Reference: (http://en.wikipedia.org/wiki/Mole_people#Cities)

867.

The world chess champion, Bobby Fischer, wouldn't have qualified for the latter stages of the process if not for another chess master giving up his spot for him.

Reference: (https://en.wikipedia.org/wiki/Bobby_Fischer#Road_to_the_World_Championship)

868.

The Great Smog of London in 1952 had acid fog combined with an anticyclone that killed 12,000 people.

Reference: (https://en.wikipedia.org/wiki/Great_Smog)

869.

There are over 10 million Manchu people but only about 10 left who still speak the Manchu language.

Reference: (https://en.wikipedia.org/wiki/Manchu_people)

870.

After 2 US officers were killed while trying to cut down a tree in the DMZ, the US and South Korea sent 813 soldiers, 27 helicopters and nuclear-capable bombers to the DMZ to supervise the cutting down of the tree. North Korean soldiers watched in silence as the tree was cut down in 42 minutes.

Reference: (http://en.wikipedia.org/wiki/Axe_murder_incident)

871.

Autistic activist, Jonathan Mitchell, says that the "Different not Disabled" view of Autism is only held by a small number of Autistics that can communicate online, providing false hope and an excuse to make profit.

Reference: (https://en.wikipedia.org/wiki/Jonathan_Mitchell#Views_on_autism_and_neurodiversity)

872.

Most mirrors are slightly green.

Reference: (http://www.livescience.com/34427-what-color-is-a-mirror.html)

873.

The English language is undergoing a sound shift in something called the Cot-caught merger; some people pronounce "cot" and "caught" the same.

Reference: (https://en.wikipedia.org/wiki/Phonological_history_of_English_low_back_vowels#Cot.E2.80.93caught_merger)

874.

There is a website that shows what the average male and female looks like from around the world.

Reference: (https://pmsol3.wordpress.com/)

875.

The Tooth Fairy was created by Spanish writer, Luis Coloma Roldan, who lived from January 9th, 1851, to April 14th, 1915.

Reference: (https://es.wikipedia.org/wiki/Luis_Coloma)

876.

The privately held Saudi Arabian Oil Company is estimated to be worth between $1.5 and $10 trillion dollars.

Reference: (https://en.wikipedia.org/wiki/Saudi_Aramco?repost)

877.

America has 19 aircraft carriers. Compared to the rest of the worlds combined 12.

Reference: (http://www.businessinsider.com/magnitude-of-us-naval-dominance-2013-11)

878.

Only 45% of the London Underground is actually underground.

Reference:
(https://en.wikipedia.org/wiki/London_Underground?repost)

879.

Now believed to be lost forever, the first ever 3D feature film was released in Los Angeles in 1922.

Reference: (http://en.wikipedia.org/wiki/3D_film)

880.

"Skinny Arm" is the name of the pose that women assume in pictures in order to diminish the abundance of flab on their inner arm.

Reference: (http://abcnews.go.com/Lifestyle/skinny-arm-met-ball-poses/story?id=23627382)

881.

A prisoner in the U.S. impregnated 4 guards and made over $15,000 per month while incarcerated.

Reference: (http://www.npr.org/blogs/thetwo-way/2013/04/24/178799235/1-inmate-impregnated-4-guards-at-md-jail-prosecutors-say)

882.

Triumph the Insult Comic Dog put out an album in 2003 called "Come Poop With Me" that featured Jack Black, Horatio Sanz, and Blackwolf the Dragonmaster.

Reference: (https://en.wikipedia.org/wiki/Come_Poop_with_Me)

883.

Twi, the most spoken language in Ghana, is taught at Fordham University in New York.

Reference:
(http://legacy.fordham.edu/campus_resources/enewsroom/topstories_1731.asp)

884.

During the Chernobyl Disaster, Aleksandr Lelechenko saved his colleagues from radiation exposure by walking through radioactive water three times in place of his younger colleagues. He died less than 2 weeks after the disaster.

Reference:
(http://en.wikipedia.org/wiki/Deaths_due_to_the_Chernobyl_disaster)

885.

Stephen King wrote "Carrie" on an old typewriter while living in a trailer. He threw away the first 3 pages thinking he had written "the world's all time loser." His wife fished the pages out and pushed him to finish it. It turned out to be his first published novel.

Reference: (http://en.wikipedia.org/wiki/Carrie_%28novel%29)

886.

A captive whale at Marine Land discovered it could regurgitate fish onto the surface of the water, attracting seagulls, and then eating the birds. Four others then learned to copy the behavior.

Reference:
(http://en.wikipedia.org/wiki/Killer_whale#Conservation)

887.

Norway knighted a penguin.

Reference:
(http://www.edinburghzoo.org.uk/animals/SirNilsOlav.html)

888.

There are large differences in average bone density between ethnic groups. For example, African Americans have the highest, followed by Caucasians and then Asian people.

Reference:
(https://depts.washington.edu/bonebio/bonAbout/race.html)

889.

Western charity clothing donations that are sent to Africa prevent its local countries from developing economies on their own.

Reference: (http://www.one.org/us/2014/03/14/what-really-happens-to-your-donated-clothing/)

890.

In 1966 and 1967, soldiers testing Agent Orange in Canada were told the chemical was completely safe and sprayed it on each other to cool off.

Reference: (http://en.wikipedia.org/wiki/Agent_Orange#Canada)

891.

The small dot on top of the latter "i" is called a "tittle".

Reference: (http://www.subtraction.com/2014/03/03/whats-the-dot-on-top-of-a-lowercase-i-called/)

892.

In 1996, ASCAP threatened to sue the Girl Scouts of America for singing campfire songs without paying licensing fees.

Reference:(http://en.wikipedia.org/wiki/American_Society_of_Composers,_Authors_and_Publishers#Criticism)

893.

Air Force One isn't a specific plane, rather it's whatever plane the president is on.

Reference: (https://en.wikipedia.org/wiki/Air_Force_One)

894.

Nepal is trying to promote Mount Everest as a gay wedding destination.

Reference:
(http://www.telegraph.co.uk/news/worldnews/asia/nepal/7027736/Nepal-to-stage-gay-weddings-on-Everest.html)

895.

Traffic in central London moves at the same speed as horse-drawn carriages a century ago.

Reference:(http://www.thisislocallondon.co.uk/news/804876.london_cars_move_no_faster_than_chickens/)

896.

Heinz was caught under filling its ketchup bottles and was ordered to overfill the bottles for the next year.

Reference: (http://www.breakingnews.ie/business/teaspoon-of-ketchup-costs-heinz-half-a-million-13912.html)

897.

For about 70 days in 1871, the people of Paris were independent from France and ruled themselves with Marxist ideals. The French National Guard had to recapture Paris.

Reference: (https://en.wikipedia.org/wiki/Paris_Commune)

898.

The Sydney Opera House cost 1457% over budget.

Reference:
(https://en.wikipedia.org/wiki/Sydney_Opera_House#Completion_and_cost)

899.

Ireland did everything it could to help the Allies in World War II, short of declaring war, and this wasn't widely known until the early 1990s.

Reference: (https://www.youtube.com/watch?v=onlGWRXkZv0)

900.

A cancer causing gene used to be called Pokémon, which is an acronym for, "POK erythroid myeloid ontogenic factor," until Nintendo sued the research company that had come up with the name; not wanting the bad press inherent with its trademark sharing a name with the gene.

Reference: (http://www.cnet.com/news/pokemon-usa-threat-leads-to-gene-name-change/)

901.

An Indian man whose wife slipped on a narrow trail destroyed the mountain it was on by hand to avoid such incidents ever happening again.

Reference: (http://archive.indianexpress.com/Storyold/1981/)

902.

A Pakistani squash player, Jahangir Khan, won 555 matches consecutively. This is the longest winning streak by any athlete in top-level professional sports as recorded by the Guinness World Records.

Reference: (https://en.wikipedia.org/wiki/Jahangir_Khan)

903.

When an attack from Acute Glaucoma takes place, you have a few hours to seek treatment or eye sight can be permanently destroyed. Many of these attacks occur in darkened places, like movie theatres.

Reference:
(https://www.glaucomafoundation.org/acute_glaucoma.htm)

904.

When Grigori Perelman, a Russian mathematician, solved the most important problem in topology he was awarded the Fields Medal and Millennium Prize of one million dollars. He declined both saying: "The main reason is my disagreement with the organized mathematical community. I don't like their decisions, I consider them unjust."

Reference: (http://en.wikipedia.org/wiki/Grigori_Perelman)

905.

President Johnson, out of respect for his assassinated predecessor, John F. Kennedy, used the Oval Office only as a formal setting with visitors and continued to do most of his work in his vice presidents suite, located in the Old Executive Office Building.

Reference:(http://www.realclearpolitics.com/articles/2013/02/01/2nd_oval_office_readied_in_white_house_rehab_project__116887.html#ixzz3jBgVP0xw)

906.

Alexander Hamilton was born in the West Indies and moved to America as a teenager, fought valiantly against the British in the Revolution, spoke Hebrew and could recite the Ten Commandments in their native language. He also had a son who was killed in a duel three years before him.

Reference: (https://en.wikipedia.org/wiki/Alexander_Hamilton)

907.

A Pakistani squash player, Jahangir Khan, won 555 matches consecutively. This is the longest winning streak by any athlete in top-level professional sports as recorded by the Guinness World Records.

Reference: (https://en.wikipedia.org/wiki/Jahangir_Khan)

908.

Italian Dictator Benito Mussolini gained a teaching certificate in 1901 and was a teacher until 1902.

Reference: (http://www.biography.com/people/benito-mussolini-9419443#impassioned-socialist)

909.

Meal breaks aren't required in most states in the United States. In fact, less than half of U.S. states require a 30 minute meal break.

Reference: (http://www.nolo.com/legal-encyclopedia/meal-rest-breaks-rights-employee-29773.html)

910.

California's official state animal is extinct.

Reference: (http://en.wikipedia.org/wiki/California_grizzly_bear)

911.

The look for Mad Magazine's famous mascot, Alfred E. Neuman, was based on 19th century anti-Irish propaganda.

Reference: (http://www.toledoblade.com/Art/2008/01/20/Mad-for-Alfred-A-new-exhibit-shows-Mad-magazine-s-poster-boy-has-a-shadowy-past.html)

912.

"Videotape" used to be a trademark.

Reference: (http://ethw.org/Ampex_Corporation)

913.

There was not only one Soviet space shuttle, but two.

Reference: (https://en.wikipedia.org/wiki/Ptichka_(Buran-class_spacecraft))

914.

A brand new console game in Australia costs 60% more than a brand new console game in the United States. The average new PS3 game in Australia costs $99 USD as opposed to $60 USD in the United States.

Reference: (http://www.kotaku.com.au/2010/11/why-do-videogames-cost-so-much/)

915.

Scientist, Louis Slotin, died while working on the Manhattan Project. He accidentally dropped a hemisphere of beryllium on a plutonium core; witnesses saw glowing blue light and felt a heat wave. He died nine days later. The plutonium core was later nicknamed the "demon core".

Reference:
(http://en.wikipedia.org/wiki/Louis_Slotin#Criticality_accident)

916.

When the Phoenix Suns joined the NBA in 1968, they had several partial owners such as Tony Curtis, Janet Leigh, Henry Mancini and Bobbi Gentry.

Reference:
(http://archive.azcentral.com/sports/suns/articles/20120927original-phoenix-suns-ownership-serious-star-power.html)

917.

The largest armed conflict on U.S. soil since the Civil War happened in 1921 between 10,000 armed coal miners and 3,000 lawmen. Over 1 million rounds were fired and the battle was only broken up after the U.S. Army became involved.

Reference: (https://en.wikipedia.org/wiki/Battle_of_Blair_Mountain)

918.

The only Academy Award that Star Trek: First Contact was nominated for was Best Makeup, but it lost to The Nutty Professor.

Reference:
(https://en.wikipedia.org/wiki/69th_Academy_Awards#Awards)

919.

Spiders tune their webs like guitars and pluck their string to separate potential food from potential mates.

Reference: (http://aeon.co/video/science/spiders-tune-their-webs-like-guitars-vibration-virtuosos/)

920.

There is an episode of Supernatural in which the two main characters are sent to an alternate universe in which they play the actors that play their characters on Supernatural (themselves) who are in the middle of filming an episode of a TV show called Supernatural.

Reference: (http://www.avclub.com/tvclub/supernatural-the-french-mistake-52323)

921.

Pixar started as a hardware company whose core product was the Pixar Image Computer, a Alan Greenspan, the former chairman of the Federal Reserve Board, married Andrea Mitchell, the NBC News correspondent, on April 6th, 1997.

Reference: (http://www.nytimes.com/1997/04/06/style/alan-greenspan-andrea-mitchell.html)

922.

Four teenage girls lied to have an innocent man convicted of murdering a child. After they were found out, they never apologized, claiming that they did it "for a laugh".

Reference:
(https://en.wikipedia.org/wiki/Murder_of_Lesley_Molseed)

923.

Tax day in the United States never falls on a Friday.

Reference: (https://en.wikipedia.org/wiki/Tax_Day)

924.

There was a sequel to the Charlie and the Chocolate Factory book in which Willy Wonka and Charlie help the United States Government fend off an attack from murderous, shape shifting aliens.

Reference: (http://allreaders.com/book-review-summary/charlie-and-the-great-glass-elevator-39833)

925.

The Dubai Mall has more visitors annually than the entirety of New York City.

Reference: (https://en.wikipedia.org/wiki/The_Dubai_Mall)

926.

The man who attempted to assassinate Ronald Reagan in 1981 was trying to impress Jodie Foster. He became obsessed with her after watching the movie "Taxi Driver."

Reference: (https://en.wikipedia.org/wiki/John_Hinckley%2C_Jr.)

927.

The United States Navy's new anti-sub aircraft is a Boeing 737 that can launch Harpoon missiles, depth charges and even a light torpedo from 30,000 feet.

Reference: (https://en.wikipedia.org/wiki/Boeing_P-8_Poseidon#Specifications_.28P-8A.29)

928.

The Good Year Blimp made a special guest appearance in the 1985 "Stop the Madness" anti-drug music video.

Reference: (https://www.youtube.com/watch?v=Z5zJvX3pIY4&t=4m49s)

929.

Liberty, President Gerald Ford's dog, was trained to create diversions in meetings. If Ford wanted to end a conversation in the Oval Office, he would signal Liberty and she would go to the guest wagging her tail, creating a natural break.

Reference: (https://en.wikipedia.org/wiki/Liberty_(dog))

930.

Dolphins don't drink water because sea water would make them sick and, possibly, kill them. Because of this, they can't differentiate between hunger and thirst.

Reference: (http://us.whales.org/whales-and-dolphins/facts-about-dolphins)

931.

During World War I, Dominic "Fats" McCarthy was awarded the Victoria Cross after he, virtually unaided, killed 22 Germans, captured 5 machine guns, 50 prisoners, and half a kilometer of the German front. When it was over, even the prisoners he'd captured patted him on the back for what he'd done.

Reference: (http://adb.anu.edu.au/biography/mccarthy-lawrence-dominic-7307)

932.

A New York window washer survived a 47 foot fall by using the platform and managed a full recovery right after.

Reference: (http://www.nytimes.com/2008/01/04/nyregion/04fall.html?pagewanted&_r=0)

933.

The character of Major Tom in David Bowie's "Space Oddity" had his story told over several decades by multiple artists, and ended in Bowie's last music video, "Blackstar".

Reference: (https://en.wikipedia.org/wiki/Major_Tom)

934.

There was a real team of Jewish assassins who called themselves "the Avengers" who organized after World War II to track down and execute Nazi war criminals.

Reference: (http://en.wikipedia.org/wiki/Nakam)

935.

According to the Peter Principe, anything that works will be used in progressively more challenging applications until it fails. Applied to a workplace, this means that "every employee tends to rise to their level of incompetence".

Reference: (http://en.wikipedia.org/wiki/Peter_Principle)

936.

Pope Benedict IX was elected Pope at the age of 20, and was the only man to ever hold the office several times. He was expelled from Rome twice and eventually was paid to abdicate.

Reference: (https://en.wikipedia.org/wiki/Pope_Benedict_IX)

937.

You can play Wizard of Oz and Dark Side of the Moon at the same time as the album and the movie are in complete sync. This was unintentional and it's called "Dark Side of the Rainbow."

Reference:
(https://en.wikipedia.org/wiki/Dark_Side_of_the_Rainbow)

938.

The conquest of British Somaliland was Italy's only victory, without the cooperation of German troops, in World War II against the Allies.

Reference:
(https://en.wikipedia.org/wiki/History_of_Somaliland#British_Soma liland)

939.

Cougar, puma and mountain lion are all different names for the same animal.

Reference: (http://en.wikipedia.org/wiki/Cougar)

940.

Brides normally stand on the left of the Groom at a wedding so that his sword hand is free to defend against any other suitors.

Reference: (https://www.theknot.com/content/must-the-bride-stand-on-the-left)

941.

If we detonated a hydrogen bomb containing all the deuterium in all the water on Earth, the blast would be powerful enough to create a black hole.

Reference:
(https://en.wikipedia.org/wiki/Micro_black_hole#Manmade_micro_black_holes)

942.

Tokyo is setting up an entire robotic village for the 2020 Olympics.

Reference: (http://www.techinsider.io/tokyo-olympics-will-be-all-about-robots-2015-10)

943.

11% of Americans think HTML is an STD.

Reference: (http://articles.latimes.com/2014/mar/04/business/la-fi-tn-1-10-americans-html-std-study-finds-20140304)

944.

Research published in Chemical Senses tested the effect of diet on male odor. 17 men ate either a meat or a meat-free diet for 2 weeks then they had their odor rated by 30 women. They then switched diets and had their odor rated again. The women rated the non-meat odors as being more attractive.

Reference: (http://www.ncbi.nlm.nih.gov/pubmed/16891352)

945.

Scientists created a completely enclosed, artificial environment called Biosphere 2 and made one mistake that caused all the trees to fall down before maturation: there was no wind so trees failed to develop stress wood, which is necessary for them to stand.

Reference: (http://travisma.wordpress.com/2013/12/12/the-necessity-of-stress/)

946.

According to a study done in 1969, the United States has had the bloodiest and most violent labor history of any industrial nation in the world.

Reference:(https://en.wikipedia.org/wiki/List_of_worker_deaths_in_United_States_labor_disputes)

947.

20 pounds of eggplant contains as much nicotine as a cigarette.

Reference:
(http://en.wikipedia.org/wiki/Eggplant#Health_properties)

948.

On May 18th, 2012, all the royal monarchs of the world gathered at Windsor Castle for a photo.

Reference:
(http://www.royaltymonarchy.com/sovereigns/0000world.html)

949.

The sound of TIE fighters from Star Wars are derived from mixing an elephant's screams with a car driving on a wet road.

Reference:
(https://en.wikipedia.org/wiki/TIE_fighter#Origin_and_design)

950.

The leading zipper brand, YKK, was fined €150 million euros for running not one, but four zipper price fixing cartels.

Reference: (http://europa.eu/rapid/press-release_IP-07-1362_en.htm?locale=en)

951.

Alcohol is an endocrine disruptor.

Reference: (http://pubs.niaaa.nih.gov/publications/aa26.htm)

952.

After "shake it like a Polaroid" became part of a hit song, Polaroid warned customers that this could actually destroy their photographs.

Reference:
(http://www.cnn.com/2004/TECH/ptech/02/17/polaroid.warns.reut/index.html)

953.

Edward Teller, who designed the Hydrogen bomb, proposed a 10 gigaton nuclear bomb called the Sundial.

Reference: (http://blog.nuclearsecrecy.com/2012/09/12/in-search-of-a-bigger-boom/)

954.

There is an ancient temple in Ireland that predates Giza and Stonehenge. During the winter solstice, light penetrates through to the burial tomb for about 19 minutes.

Reference: (http://newgrange.com/)

955.

Most Hindus believe that euthanasia interrupts the timing of the cycle of rebirth and both the doctor and patient will take on bad karma as a result.

Reference:
(http://www.bbc.co.uk/religion/religions/hinduism/hinduethics/euthanasia.shtml)

956.

Notorious English pirate captain Benjamin Hornigold, once attacked a ship off the coast of Honduras just to replace his crew's hats, as they had drunkenly lost them the night before.

Reference:
(https://en.wikipedia.org/wiki/Benjamin_Hornigold#Early_career)

957.

The Fibonacci Sequence was described by an Indian mathematician, 1200 years before Fibonacci wrote of it.

Reference: (https://en.wikipedia.org/wiki/Pingala)

958.

A woman woke up at her own funeral and was so shocked by it that she had a heart attack and died.

Reference: (http://unusualdeaths.com/2012/06/01/fagilyu-mukhametzyanov/)

959.

The world's most powerful nuclear powered icebreaker, which routinely visits the North Pole, can't cross the equator and sail to the southern hemisphere because the tropical waters are too warm for it to operate.

Reference: (https://en.wikipedia.org/wiki/Yamal_(icebreaker))

960.

Twin brothers ran a marathon. Halfway through the race, they switched places in a toilet. The 1st brother drove ahead while his twin ran, rejoining the race ahead and finished 9th. They were caught once a journalist noticed that the two wore their watches on opposite hands in different pictures.

Reference: (http://www.sahistory.org.za/dated-event/south-african-athlete-sergio-motsoeneng-admits-cheating-comrades-marathon)

961.

The German Parliament building has a glass dome above it that people can walk over. This was done to remind the politicians that the government should be transparent and that the people are always above them.

Reference: (http://en.wikipedia.org/wiki/Reichstag_dome)

962.

The Japanese count in sets of 10,000 not 1,000 as we do in the West.

Reference: (http://www.trussel.com/jnumbers.htm)

963.

The taco was invented by the original inhabitants of Mexico. Fillings in tacos included fish, locusts, snails and, in some locations, live insects.

Reference:
(http://whatscookingamerica.net/History/Tortilla_Taco_history.htm)

964.

After Mark Twain met Helen Keller at a dinner party, he was so impressed with her that he wrote to the wife of Henry H. Rogers, a wealthy oil magnate, pleading with her to convince her husband to support Keller's education. Mr. Rogers agreed and personally paid for her entire education.

Reference: (http://historyofredding.com/epl/twain-keller-exhibit1.htm)

965.

Researchers determined that 'deer crossing' warning signs do not prevent accidents.

Reference: (http://www.wibw.com/home/headlines/2798616.html)

966.

A California hospital charges $223,000 for joint replacement surgery that costs $5,300 in Oklahoma.

Reference: (http://thecontributor.com/health-care/ca-hospital-charges-223000-joint-replacement-costs-5300-ok)

967.

Fornication between unmarried, consenting individuals is a Class 4 Misdemeanor in Virginia.

Reference: (https://vacode.org/18.2-344/)

968.

In 1980, the British Government invested a million pounds into an anti-smoking campaign featuring Superman fighting "Nick-OTeen".

Reference:
(http://www.screenonline.org.uk/film/id/1396646/index.html)

969.

A New York window washer survived a 47 feet fall by using the platform and managed a full recovery right after.

Reference:
(http://www.nytimes.com/2008/01/04/nyregion/04fall.html?pagewan
ted&_r=0)

970.

Patrice Lumumba, the first democratically elected PM of Congo and
pan-Africanist, lasted only 81 days before being killed by the
Belgians and the CIA.

Reference: (http://en.wikipedia.org/wiki/Patrice_Lumumba)

971.

There exists a religion called Dudeism, based on The Big
Lebowsky's Dude's way of life.

Reference: (http://en.wikipedia.org/wiki/Dudeism)

972.

In high school, John Malkovich lost 70 pounds by putting himself on
a diet of only Jell-O for three months.

Reference: (http://www.edrive.com/edrive03/celebs/john-
malkovich/index.html)

973.

The Korean population of Kazakhstan increased by more than 2,000
times between 1926 and 1939.

Reference:
(https://en.wikipedia.org/wiki/Demographics_of_Kazakhstan)

974.

Banana ketchup is popular in the Philippines.

Reference: (http://en.wikipedia.org/wiki/Banana_ketchup)

975.

Afrika Bambata was one of the founding pioneers of hip hop music. He reformed his own and several other New York street gangs into the culture based organization, the Universal Zulu Nation, with the goal of stopping violence and spreading the values of hip hop based on peace, unity, love and having fun.

Reference:
(https://www.youtube.com/watch?v=2w2axPEbJb4&feature=youtu.be)

976.

Kids Wish Foundation was named America's Worst Charity. Only 3 cents of every dollar raised went to the actual cause.

Reference: (http://www.tampabay.com/americas-worst-charities/charities/kids-wish-network-inc)

977.

Elizabeth Fraser, formerly of the Cocteau Twins, is the vocalist on Massive Attack's "Teardrop" song and considers the song to be a tribute to her late friend, Jeff Buckley, who passed away during the recording process.

Reference:
(https://en.wikipedia.org/wiki/Teardrop_(song)#Development)

978.

The term "weather forecast" was coined by a 19th century naval captain; the same one who took Charles Darwin on his famous voyage in 1931. After he committed suicide, Darwin contributed £100 to a fund set up for his wife and daughter.

Reference: (https://en.wikipedia.org/wiki/Robert_FitzRoy)

979.

The French mathematician, Abraham de Moivre, predicted the date of his own death by noticing he slept an extra 15 minutes each day.

Reference: (https://en.wikipedia.org/wiki/Abraham_de_Moivre)

980.

The world's largest beaver dam is 850 meters or 2,800 feet long. Its ecological impact in a remote part of Alberta, Canada is visible from space, which is how it was discovered.

Reference: (http://phys.org/news/2010-05-world-biggest-beaver-northern-canada.html)

981.

The Simplified Spelling Board, created in 1906 by a Carnegie, was created due to the belief that English was becoming a universal language and, therefore, could lead to world peace. However, its complex spelling inhibited that.

Reference:
(https://en.wikipedia.org/wiki/Simplified_Spelling_Board)

982.

The Spiny Anteater shows no interest in mating while in captivity and, therefore, no one has even seen one ejaculate. There have been attempts, trying to force them to ejaculate through the use of electrically stimulated ejaculation, but it has only results in its penis swelling.

Reference: (https://en.wikipedia.org/wiki/Echidna#Reproduction)

983.

There is an ethnic minority in the Philippines whose life expectancy at birth is 16.5 years and, at the age of 15, is only 27.5 years.

Reference:(https://en.wikipedia.org/wiki/Aeta_people?sa=X&ved=0 ahUKEwjK7JWT_YnMAhUBxSYKHZiHC4sQ9QEIEDAA)

984.

75% of Japanese homes have a hi-tech toilet and the latest models eliminate the need for toilet paper, keep you warm, check your blood pressure, play running-water sounds to increase privacy and open and close automatically so you don't have to touch anything.

Reference: (http://www.nydailynews.com/news/national/new-high-tech-toilets-not-require-hands-paper-article-1.1710437)

985.

The United States ranks only 21st when it comes to military spending as a percentage of its GDP.

Reference:(http://data.worldbank.org/indicator/MS.MIL.XPND.GD. ZS?order=wbapi_data_value_2014+wbapi_data_value+wbapi_data_ value-last&sort=desc)

986.

Neil Young has two children with cerebral palsy by two different women, which is a statistical near-impossibility given the fact that CP is not a genetic disease.

Reference:
(https://www.youtube.com/watch?v=1Zon_1_HodQ&feature=youtu. be)

987.

German law prohibits the killing of animals without reasonable cause, therefore, kill shelters are outlawed.

Reference: (https://en.wikipedia.org/wiki/Animal_shelter#Germany)

988.

The total death tolls at Snaefell Mountain Course and Mount Everest are about the same.

Reference:(https://en.wikipedia.org/wiki/List_of_Snaefell_Mountain _Course_fatalities#List_of_fatal_accidents_involving_competitors)

989.

When the Phoenix Suns joined the NBA in 1968, they had several partial owners such as Tony Curtis, Janet Leigh, Henry Mancini and Bobbi Gentry.

Reference:
(http://archive.azcentral.com/sports/suns/articles/20120927original-phoenix-suns-ownership-serious-star-power.html)

990.

There is a Castle in the Czech Republic that has had a "Bear Moat" filled with actual bears for the past 300 years.

Reference:
(http://www.castle.ckrumlov.cz/docs/cz/zamek_oinf_sthrza.xml)

991.

The Landkreuzer P. 1000 Ratte is the biggest tank that Hitler approved before its bigger brother was imagined.

Reference:
(https://en.wikipedia.org/wiki/Landkreuzer_P._1000_Ratte)

992.

To talk to submarines, we use the Earth as an antenna because of the long wavelength.

Reference:(https://en.wikipedia.org/wiki/Extremely_low_frequency# Difficulties_of_ELF_communication)

993.

Our brains render 5% of our eye's field of view in high and sharp definition. The remainder is lower quality unfocused peripheral vision.

Reference: (https://en.wikipedia.org/wiki/Peripheral_vision)

994.

Most Europeans thought that the tomato was poisonous because of the way plates and flatware were made in the 1500s.

Reference: (http://www.tomato-cages.com/tomato-history.html)

995.

In 2011, James Franco put his name behind a project called "The Museum of Non-visible Art". A woman paid $10,000 for a non-visible piece called "Fresh Air".

Reference: (http://www.npr.org/blogs/thetwo-way/2011/07/22/138513048/woman-pays-10-000-for-non-visible-work-of-art)

996.

Most Europeans thought that the tomato was poisonous because of the way plates and flatware were made in the 1500s.

Reference: (http://www.tomato-cages.com/tomato-history.html)

997.

The Amazon River dumps so much fresh water into the Atlantic that it is possible to drink from the surface for about 200 miles offshore.

Reference:
(https://en.wikipedia.org/wiki/Amazon_River?repost#Drainage_area
)

998.

The first German serviceman killed in World War II was killed by the Japanese and the first American serviceman killed was killed by the Russians.

Reference:(http://www.military.com/NewContent/0,13190,Defensewatch_111903_Lighter,00.html)

999.

Carol of the Bells wasn't a Christmas song originally but a Ukrainian song that told of a swallow that would fly into their homes on the New Year and tell of their good fortune for the next year.

Reference: (https://en.wikipedia.org/wiki/Carol_of_the_Bells)

1000.

McDonald's offers product placement rewards to rap artists who mention the Big Mac in their songs.

Reference: (http://en.wikipedia.org/w/index.php?title=Big_Mac)

www.ingramcontent.com/pod-product-compliance
Lightning Source LLC
Chambersburg PA
CBHW051254250726
48656CB00004B/1287